# BREAKAWAY

KATHLEEN TAYLOR-BENNETT

authorHOUSE®

*AuthorHouse™*
*1663 Liberty Drive, Suite 200*
*Bloomington, IN 47403*
*www.authorhouse.com*
*Phone: 1-800-839-8640*

*First published by AuthorHouse 10/8/2007*

*ISBN: 978-1-4343-4294-2 (sc)*

*Printed in the United States of America*
*Bloomington, Indiana*

*This book is printed on acid-free paper.*

I would like to dedicate this book to my mother Anester (Ms. Ann) Hall and my Angelic father, the late John Lincoln Taylor both of Vicksburg, Ms from whom I received my strength, wisdom, and wit. To Anthony, thank "GOD" for the precious angel given to you as your wife; you are beyond blessed to have me and would be more than a fool to lose me! To my son Sheann, your "hard head" helps to keep me strong, to my son Anthony Jr, your indecisiveness helps keep me on point, and to my beautiful daughter Taylor, you are my biggest supporter in all I do and I'm partly who I am because of you. To my eight sisters and two brothers, Threasa (Tina) Hall, Jovita (Hobe) Hall, Perri "Renee" & (James) Johnson, Traci Heath, and Johnni (Joni) Taylor all of Vicksburg, Ms; Erica D. Taylor of Lockport, NY, and Gwendolyn (Gwen) Hogan of Jackson, Ms, Dexter & (Penny P) Hall of Milwaukie, Or formerly of Portland, Or and Clarence (Speedy) Hall of Louisiana. I know I am truly blessed to have all you freaks in my life because you make even me seem less crazy at times! I Love you all! I would also like to acknowledge my many nieces and nephews who always keep me smiling, laughing and joking. To my best friends Natasha (Nat) Derby-West of Vicksburg, Ms and Kimberly Smith-Turner of Atlanta, Ga…Thank you for allowing me to lean on you in my times of need; Nat…you and Gwen are truly my rocks! To Dr. Philip L.S., I am so very grateful for your continued help…Thank you. To all you "real" women out there who have not made it to the Promised Land in your marriage or relationship, keep your heads up and stay the course; it awaits you on the other side of your man's lies. Also, to you boys, who find enjoyment in a creep, don't be surprised or angered when your woman's needs a real man starts to meet! I hope my truthful poignancy in the words of this book hit's you "boys" where it hurts the most; it's my honest gift to you. Enjoy!

Other Books By This Author:

Human Emotions: A Book of Poetry

Breakaway; what does that mean to a woman who has given all of herself, faithfully in a relationship? More times than not, it means a woman has finally let go of her equator; that imaginary line that separates her from her pride, common sense, and self respect. It means she has finally chosen to be happy rather than to be in a relationship or situation to put it more honestly. As women, we all too often feel as if we have to endure whatever is thrown our way to keep the man, or boy, in our lives happy. We ask ourselves, "Why do I continue to go through this?" "Why do I continue to allow him to treat me this way and not leave?" Because we are loving and forgiving individuals by nature, we often put everyone else's needs before our own and are not the type of people to give up on anything without a fight. We often forget about our own needs and end up in a self-defeating situation that only serves to further diminish our self-worth and self-respect. We allow ourselves to be put on a path of self-destruction and self-sacrificing behavior because we allow guilt to come into play and overrule everything we know to be right. By forgetting who we are, we forge ourselves into the person our other half wants us to be instead of whom we know ourselves to be. We become completely engulfed in what "he" needs and what "he" wants and suffer the consequences of a self-recriminating attitude which leads to self-hate and self-loathing, so much so that we can no longer tell where he ends and we begin! The single life; it sounds like the perfect life unless you're one of the people in it. We as women want to be in a relationship. We crave and long to be part of a "couple." We love to be held, cuddled, and told how much we are loved and how beautiful we are. We seem to be miserable unless we have a man in our life; a man to call our own. We go out on date after date, go to party after party until we have found that perfect man; or what we at the time believe to be the perfect man. We are so smitten and taken in by his charm, the way he treats us, the way he opens the door for us, the way he gives us the umbrella while he runs in the rain to bring the vehicle to us that we are just totally mesmerized by this man. We talk about him so much that our friends and family feel like they're dating him! You can't wait to call each other on the phone, when someone has actually peeled you two apart, six and seven times a day because you have so much to talk about and you two have so much in common that it must have been fate that sent him to you. You start telling your friends "this is the one, I know it; we're perfect for each other!" It's been a whirlwind three or four weeks and you two decide that you want to be exclusive. You're a couple now; you're in a relationship and all seems to be right with the world. It sounds like a nursery rhyme, but it's your life. It has been an amazing six months together so far. The only thing you two have had to fuss about was who was going to leave the tip after that wonderful Chinese dinner you two just had. You just can't believe how much you two have in common! You have decided that it's time for you two to get married and move in together. If your time together so far has been this perfect, it can only get better. Your friends, you know the ones you say are always bringing you down, advise you to slow down and just continue dating; you're both still young and you have plenty of time to move in together; after all, you've only been together six months! You will hear of no such nonsense! You two are madly in love, you have similar goals in life, and something that made you love him even more than you thought possible was when he told you that he wanted kids. You would trust him with your life! That was the icing on the cake; right then and there you knew it couldn't get any better. That was your dream, to be in a wonderful and stable relationship and to have the children that you love so much. You feel your friends have your best interest at heart, but they don't know him like you do. They don't get to see the loving and kind man behind the wonderful man. Your mind is made up; you two will soon be a real couple, living together and starting a family. It's been another couple months and you two have found the perfect apartment. You two move in together and it is pure bliss. You both have good jobs, money in the bank, and enjoy every waking moment you two spend together. The date is set, the arrangements are made, and you have just lived your fairy tail wedding. You can't imagine anything making you happier than becoming his wife. Your lives have been going so perfectly that you feel it's time to think about having kids; he feels just as strongly as you do and the two of you begin to try for that little miss or that Jr. After an exhaustive, but pleasant year, you two have finally been blessed. You're finally pregnant! You have the most enjoyable pregnancy with your true love, both your families and friends doting over you and the baby. You have that "glow" that makes pregnancy seem like winning the lottery; nothing can compare. Oh, this can't be true; you have just received the most amazing news from your doctor…twins! How could two people be more blessed than to have two babies at once. Two tiny little people that you already love more than you ever thought you were capable of. You're counting down the days; it's time for your little treasures to meet their parents and the world. You find yourself on the delivery table, in excruciating pain, but looking forward to seeing and holding your babies. They are so adorable and cameras are flashing as if the paparazzi has just entered your room. You get all the medical information you need and it's only been a couple of days, but you're back in the privacy and luxury of your own home. It's been a couple of months and things have been going perfectly until you call his cell phone and a woman answers. Your mind is racing, your heart is beating faster and faster, you can't breathe; you're wondering what the hell is going on. Who was that person? Where is my husband? Could he be cheating on me? He comes home three hours later to answer all those questions by saying, "we need to talk." That big fat bully called life has just stepped in your pathway, refusing to move, and knocked the wind out of you with a huge fist to the chest; that bullies' name…"reality"! My best friend Nat jokingly says I have a crazy way with words when I use metaphors in this way; let's just hope they shake you up enough to wake you up. He says he loves you and the kids more than life itself, but admits to seeing another woman for the past three months! "It just happened" he says; like he's saying he got a promotion or he decided to take a vacation. He makes light of the situation, but your heart, spirit, mind, and trust is broken. Where do you go from here? What are you supposed to say to that? What is your next move? This is my short, summarized version of a two or three year courtship. It's an abridged example of how beautiful it can begin and how ugly it can end. I would like to offer up some personal advice if the above scenario sounds even remotely similar to something you've gone through or are currently going through. I'm speaking for women inside the glass, and I have been there a time or two in my thirty four years here, looking to get out. A lot of you, that were lucky enough to make it out, are now looking, with sympathy, inside the glass of other women that's being shattered from within by the dishonesty of a man. Statistics, atleast the ones I've viewed, say that anywhere from forty to sixty percent of married men will stray, a cute little word for breaking their vows and cheating, within the span of their marriage. Studies, you know the ones you are never a part of and only read about, also say men cheat when they're marriage is already in trouble; baloney, and not the sandwich meat either! That is nothing more than a cop-out for men to do their dirt! Why is it when the marriage is in trouble and he cheats, he's the only one that knew there was a problem with the marriage? I often wonder why men cheat, lie, have misplaced loyalty and are just all out dogs. A man being called a "dog" may seem like a cliché but the truth is that some of them rightfully earn that title. I have witnessed, and have felt the sting myself a couple times, a man take a wonderful relationship with a woman and sometimes kids and throw it all away for a quick roll in the sack with a trashy female! This subject is a bit touchy for me because I don't understand why a man has to lie and cheat to feel like a real man. I guess their feeble little minds have them believe that to love and honor "one" woman makes them less of a man and more of what other men like to call "whipped!" I have seen good men, influenced so much by their single and or obviously unhappy friends, turn a wholesome, well-balanced home into a circus. Once these men have that "man to man talk" with one of their loser friends, they no longer show the same love, respect, honesty, compassion or loyalty towards their family or the woman that they have pledged their love to; they milk the relationship for all it's worth and wonder why some of us woman decide to leave or even play the cheating game with them. I know an eye for an eye is not the way to handle a cheating man, especially in this day of AIDS and HIV, but a broken heart can make a woman do some strange things. Women sometimes find themselves in denial about what they know is going on right under their noses. I guess they think if they ignore it, like a headache, it will eventually go away. Ladies this is not a headache, atleast not in literal terms; what's happening to you will not just go away, it will only get worse! For those of us that get mad as hell at the very thought that our man could be cheating and call him on it, please do not settle for that lame "I'm not doing anything, there you go with that thinking again, you're going to believe what you want to anyway so I don't have anything to say, or nothing is going on," a lie! What they really mean to say is that they will never do it again and get caught! Some men will break it off with the skank if they get caught or are close to being caught, I use that term because she doesn't deserve to be called a woman, because she's now more trouble than she's worth. She is now dead vermin to him, but trust me when I tell you he has definitely started looking for live bait. Men love to call you "crazy" when you're too close to finding out about the other woman or women; some of them never seem to be satisfied, and will continue stepping out on you with these other women. Trust me you're not crazy, you've just avoided that trail of red herrings he threw out at you. His friends, pretending to be helpful towards you, will try and throw you off his trail by laying out a few red herrings as well, but continue to follow your instincts because if it is telling you something is wrong, it most likely is. Men will also have you believe the affair(s) that they are having or have had were your fault!

They will have the ordasity to say "well you kept accusing me so I went ahead and did it" or "we were not getting along at the time and it just happened." Can I package bullshit and market it to see if it will sell because he is living in some psychedelic reality all his own it has him trippin big time? Like you actually said to him "if you don't go out and have an affair right now our marriage is over;" in such a sick, twisted, and never happening case, it would definitely then be your fault! Tell me, how many times would you have to get knocked in the head to give him permission to cheat on you? I don't think it's humanly possible to survive that many blows to the head. Oh and don't they look stupid when they're caught with no explanation, like they've forgotten how to speak English…uhm, I uh, we were just, this is not what it looks like! What fruit truck did he just fall off of to think you would believe that lie? Let's talk a little about what I call "the change" men go through for a minute. I have seen the damage that is done when a man goes from calling his wife or significant other cute little names like baby, honey, sweetheart, sweetie, sugar and all the other goo-goo gah-gah names to calling her stupid, ignorant, dumb, worthless bitches, tired whores and a host of other names they would cringe and turn into the hulk to hear someone call their mother, sister, or daughter! I have to say, my least favorite is when they get on the subject of weight and call their mates fat and lazy slobs after they have given them the precious gift of children and are no longer the size four or a six that they fell in love with; they now wear a sizeable, drum roll please…ten. Did I just say ten? Is that allowed? Am I going to get into trouble? Well call me crazy, but it's obvious after this that he fell in love with the physical and not the mental you! You now actually have curves and a figure and you're being called what you are nowhere near which is fat! It just burns my corneas looking at them with such disgust that I could shoot heat seeking beams from my eyes and burn them into a nice little pile of ashes and sweep them up like the trash they are! Now I know that's not humanly possible, but the thought alone makes me feel a little better since you can't just walk up to them and cut their tongues out for the very nasty things they have grown accustomed to saying! Why, instead of help and encouragement if their wife feels she needs it and wants to lose weight, would the man that pledged his life to you for better or worse even have those thoughts in his head and allow them to roll of his tongue? Oh, and for the record let me just say, that fake hula-hoop, spare tire sized belt of fat around your waists looking like a baby of nine, sometimes twelve, months waiting to be born, and those "bigger than mine" breasts, and non-muscular body are not attractive to us on your fat asses either men! Men seem to have lost all sense of what a real relationship is when they feel like they have given too much of themselves, but expect us woman to give twice as much and not gripe about anything. Why after putting so many years, tears, love and trust into a relationship and building a strong foundation would a man all of a sudden want to tear it down because they feel like they're "losing themselves" is a mystery to me; that's also their weak line, not mine! I can just punch them in their lying mouths when they use that weak line to be able to act like a single man again while their wives come home from work and cook, clean, wash clothes, take care of the kids, run all the errands, pay the bills, balance the checkbook and still find time to give to them; too much for any one person to have to do alone. These men are also more inclined to become physically violent with you, especially since they are already verbally and emotionally abusive. My advice to you; GET OUT! There's never really a legitimate reason to hit a woman; albeit, it's a different story if you're cornered and she has a razor sharp machete whaling it at you like a mad woman, and because that's your only way out, you give her one good lick or shove to get away. How likely is that to happen though? Without any sort of statistics in hand, I feel comfortable saying that it's very unlikely to happen. Also, if it does, you probably won't want to do again what made her that upset in the first place because I'm sure it was more than likely "you" that started the altercation. I have two sons, two brothers, nephews, and male cousins so I have to allow some leeway for a few men. However, if I find out they have hit a woman and I don't see that machete, then we will have one serious problem with them on the receiving end! I won't take it so I don't condone it. Hit me and I'm going to strike you back! Becoming physically violent with your spouse is unacceptable behavior. My best advice to you men that find yourself on the giving end of your wife as a punching bag is to consider if that were your mother, daughter, sister, niece, or other female family member; would you like to see how they look after a couple rounds with their ring partner? I highly doubt you would. I consider these men to be cowards and worthless losers for having something so wonderful and tossing it aside like used trash! I have seen women give up jobs and all their pride to make a man, who does not deserve them, happy while they are miserable and feel helpless to do anything about it except to take it! Women get to the point where asking their husband a simple question like "are you going out again tonight" stop bothering to ask because he will become outraged and verbally insulting in such a way that they just keep their mouths closed, wait and see. What kind of a life is that for a woman to have to live? Why does she have to give up being who she is, to make a man who doesn't care about her feelings, happy? Women, being naturally nurturing beings, feel like we have to keep the peace; we have to be the glue that holds our family's foundation together and we are willing to sacrifice almost anything, even our own happiness, to make it work. Men, however, can gut a relationship in such a way that there is only a hollow shell of what it once was left. We as women turn inward and hide the pain of what our lives are really like and show the world what we think they want to see. We become so ashamed and embarrassed that we live the lie that is forced upon us until we become a shell of our former selves, and in doing that we become so dependent on this broken relationship that we believe we have no other choice but to stay. We believe we can't start over; well ladies all it takes is a little want to make it happen. When a man's dishonesty becomes who he is, we think we don't have many choices about what our next move should be. We contemplate leaving but we think to ourselves "he's the bread winner of the family so how will I start over and take care of the kids?" I say, just do it! If it has gotten so bad that you feel like you're suffocating and drowning then the best thing for you, and the kids if you have any, is to get out! There are laws in place that are there to protect your interests and the interest of any children you may have. I know, from experience, that doing that is easier said than done but what's the alternative? Continue to live a life that makes you and your children miserable? Continue to live a lie so people won't talk? Stay in a relationship that could end in tragedy for you and your kids? Well guess what, people are going to talk regardless, good or bad, so that is something we women just need to deal with. We don't have to stand for being treated like anything less than a lady. We have the right to live a normal, happy, and healthy life with someone who loves us for who we are. Someone who has buried the "playboy" within for good! Also, when there are children involved, you have to think of their well-being before your own and get them out of that situation as quickly as possible. Misplaced loyalty; why does this happen? When your man says things to you like "my buddy is going through a tough time right now and I need to be there for him because he'd do the same for me." What the hell does he mean by that? What happened to that same level of loyalty when you had those c-sections giving birth to his child but he could never find the time to be at home to help you? What happened to that loyalty when your child had a fever of 104 but he still had to go to work because he didn't feel like he could afford to miss a day? What happened to that loyalty when you lost a family member or a close friend and he said "he couldn't stand to see you hurt in such a way so he had to leave because he didn't know how to comfort you?" Men sometimes have testicles as big as coconuts when it comes to some of the things they do and say! Men would have you believe that you are cold-hearted or just plain heartless when they can't be with that so called "ailing buddy" the way they believe they should be able to. Men are the ones that can be cold-blooded and heartless! Another "man-thing" that gets under my skin; when they have to leave out of the house at 10:00 pm "claiming" to put gas in the car for the next day! Now why couldn't they put that gas in the vehicle on the way home from work or leave out ten minutes earlier the next day and put gas in the vehicle? Men, do you actually think we believe you? Well, take heed…we don't! Another one is when they have to go to the store, alone, thirty minutes after you have just gotten back from the store, asking before you left if he needed anything and he said no! You both have cell phones and he's at home, but he just remembered what he needed or wanted as you were pulling into the driveway. Do they actually think we don't know what the hell they're doing? They come back, an hour and a half later mind you, with some odor eaters for their sneakers that are not required for work the next morning! Oh, this one is a doozey; yeah, I used that word! When they come home from work seemingly so tired and flustered wanting to just kick back and relax all to get a call on their cell phones and have to take a shower, put on fresh clothing, cologne, and their nice jewelry and say they are going to try and help their buddy fix his car that cut off on the freeway! Isn't it also strange that neither your husband nor his buddy ever answers their phones until your husband is five minutes from walking in the door? Your husband, after ten or twenty calls to his cell, answers and says "he should be home any minute; it took us a little longer than we thought!" Can you just imagine yourself drop kicking both of them in the face and blackening their eyes? I sure can! I believe men actually think we believe it when they tell us these incredible stories. I believe they think we live in this alternate universe where we can't think for ourselves and they can tell us the sky is pink and green and we actually see it that way. What do WE do when they tell us these lies? We suck it up and say ok, knowing they are leaving the house to do something they have no business doing. There is a saying that I really believe to be true. It says "If you are doing something that you can't do in the presence of your spouse or something that you know your spouse wouldn't approve of if they were there, then you know you're doing wrong!" Now if that doesn't have the ring, alarm, or siren of truth to it, then there is no such thing as the truth! Men think it's alright to flirt, often taking it to the next six levels to include explicit conversations with their female co-workers, patrons, women on the street and anywhere else a skirt swings. Some people say "a little flirting never hurt anyone", but it has; it's hurt many women. It's not that "little white lie" that never hurts anyone. We're not talking about denying who drank the last Diet Dr. Pepper. The reason behind that, I believe, is because a man does not seem to know that flirting itself is wrong and IF you're going to do it anyway, it is suppose to be joking and playful with no intentions to take it any further than those couple words...PERIOD! Men also don't understand, because most of them have shit for brains, that there is to be no continual flirting, which is what happens the majority of the time, because it leads to them cheating on their wives and destroying their marriage and the trust it once held. Another thing ladies, if your husband is a salaried employee, don't think he's spending all his eight or ten hours at work! His pay stub is going to say he's been there those eighty hours when he's actually only worked sixty hours. The hour difference I use maybe a little extreme, but you get my point. Call him on a regular basis at work. Make that call every hour to an hour and a half even if you have to punch up your reason behind doing so with "I couldn't sleep and just wanted to hear your voice" or "I'm just bored and wanted to talk" and you can always used the age old truthful line of "I need you to stop at the store and pick up these things on your way home." Never take anything at face value unless your husband has never given you a reason to doubt him. I believe there are very few of those relationships left out there so stay on guard and never say what your man won't do, is not doing, or has never done because you can be setting yourself up for a rude awakening! If you feel the slightest bit uncomfortable with what he has told you, ask questions; check his story out. It will also serve you well to get to know a few people where he works; these acquaintances will serve you well in future situations. Those same people you are to feed with a long handled spoon though; you only need to be around them when it suits your needs. I know this may sound harsh but you don't want to open yourself up to becoming "too" friendly with a male co-worker of his because you just might start to like being around him and a with the female co-worker, well lets just say she could be his reason for leaving work early. Don't be afraid to ask questions and if your man challenges you to pop-up on him if you feel the need to wherever he tells you he will be ...DO IT! It may be a change for you, but it should be a welcomed and regular one and a shock for him; use his pitiful attempt at reverse psychology against him. Now this is when it hits below the belt; when the man that you love with all your heart and promised yourself to in front of your family and most importantly GOD, comes to you after he's been caught and says "I made a mistake, why can't you just forgive me?" "We are supposed to stick together for better or for worse!" Now I would become extremely enraged and probably physically violent if my husband cheated on me and used text from the bible like he's so holy to "guilt trip" me into staying with him or to just get over it! How dare he try and make you feel like you've done something wrong! I have seen it happen and what it has done to the woman is not a pretty sight. It strips a woman of all she has known to be right and true and makes a mockery of what she believed was a happy marriage. I personally am not gullible enough, probably because I've learned that most of the time the glass is half empty, to believe there is such a thing as a perfect man or a perfect marriage. I do however believe that there is a person out there that would be perfect for each of us, but we sometimes have to get it wrong a couple times before we can finally get it right. Some of us women will spend a lifetime doing it wrong before we figure it out and by then we will have grown into bitter old women and will hold no hope that it actually could have been done right. The ones that are lucky enough to get it right the first time have been blessed more than they can imagine. Some of us strike out a couple times before we get it right, but we do so early enough to live a long and happy life with that mate that's perfect for us. Fate can be a beautiful thing that points you in the direction of real and true love or it can be such a vengeful and vindictive thing connecting you with the most despicable of men that it feels like you have been handed over to the devil only to be tortured for all eternity. Question, where along the way in your relationship, past or present, did you notice your other half, I definitely won't say better half, had stopped showing you emotion? True story, a woman I am very fond of has been having a hard time with her health lately; she has some ongoing nagging problems and some that can be potentially fatal if she isn't careful with her health. Her husband, without her knowledge, has made plans to go bowling, fishing, playing pool, or just hanging out to drink more than a few beers that adds to that ever growing baby they look to be carrying; seeing this is one of her very bad days and she feels very sick, he nonchalantly asks "are you ok" knowing she's not but she says yes anyway because she knows that if he has to stay home with her, he will resent her for it and instead of trying to help her get better, he stays away from her because he's angry that he had to change his plans to stay home with her. What a great husband right? The only thing you wouldn't trade him for is a big, hungry, and angry grizzly bear. Showing a little selflessness is impossible for them. He's rotten to the core and she still loves him enough to try and make it work. Where in the world of marriage and caring for your spouse did becoming angry because she's sick come in? I think that is very pitiful for a man to hold his wife's illnesses against her and speaks volumes for the type of person he really is. Like I said before, we women, being nurturing by nature, would have first of all not made plans without finding out what's going on in the household and then making sure it's alright with our spouses first. It's not an issue of asking permission, it's being respectful of his feelings and including him in our plans before we just decide to go scampering off into the sunset. What's so hard about saying to your spouse "have you made any plans or do you need me for anything around the house?" "The guys and I want to go and bowl a couple games at the bowling alley, we'll only be a couple hours, and I have my cell phone and you know the number to the facility; are you OK with that?" That's not asking permission or being whipped; that's showing the utmost respect for your marriage, wife, and family first and all the other non-importants second! I place so little faith or worth in a man that feels like he has to be able to come and go as he pleases in order to feel adequate as a man. I feel those types are looking to fill inadequacies that have been planted in their heads by their male friends and associates. In a marriage or a truly committed relationship, there is suppose to be give and take; men sometimes just try and take too much too often without giving anything in return. It's sad, but some men are even willing to give up their marriage to be able to live the playboy lifestyle; by that I mean they're always on the go; too anxious and worried about not being seen by outside women than worrying about their wives and children not seeing them and their marriage suffering because of it. I should correct myself and call them boys because only boys are still young, gullible, and weak minded enough to fall into those traps. No real man would ever risk his family to appease any friend, buddy, or homeboy! I have actually heard a man say that even though he loves his wife with all his heart, he doesn't know if he wants to be married because he can't do enough things outside the household with his friends and other things of that nature when he wants to; he wants to be able to just come and go as he pleases. Why not put that much effort into your relationship? I ask, why not share that time with your wife? Give her and your marriage that time away from home and the kids if you just insist on getting out the house. I know how some of you are going to respond; you'll say "she doesn't even like to do the things I like to do." I say, "and your point is?" I'm sure she won't huff and puff and blow the plans you've made for the two of you out the air. She'll leave her alter ego, The Big Bad Wolf, at home when you two leave for your outing together. Once you're married, you're supposed to give up certain bachelor attitudes for the attitude of a good and respectable husband and father. Why create a problem that you know is only going to drive an even bigger wedge between you and your spouse? Is being able to get out of your home and away from your wife important enough to end the commitment you made in front of GOD? To not be able to see your kids go to sleep at night and wake up with them in the morning knowing they are cared for and safe? Being there for them if they've have a bad day, a bad cough, or just want to be near daddy; is it really worth it? I can't imagine anything more important and loving than being there for your wife and children whenever they need you. Not that we women aren't capable of making sure they are safe and healthy because that's what we do, but why would a man want to give that up? I'll tell you why; because he's a weak minded simpleton! To group your family in the same little package as a day out with the fellas or something of that nature is ridiculously sickening. No outing or game of any magnitude should be that important to anyone unless, and that's a questionable unless, it's their career and how they support their family. We women aren't stupid; we know a big part of you wanting to go without us is because there will be plenty of hoochies that you can have your pick of, sample it, and come back home, probably with a nasty itch, acting like you were the perfect gentleman while you were away. Give me a break; and I don't mean a piece of candy bar! I say hoochies because any respectable woman would see that ring on a man's finger, or the tan line from where he took it off, and disgustingly walk away from him. Men have a knack for saying "you're always talking about what I might do or judging me by what my friends do!" Ladies, men in this case, tend to gravitate towards the same kind of person that they are or aspire to be like. As the saying goes "you live what you learn." I should also say that men want to live what their dog friends teach their simple minded asses. Even as an adult that saying still holds true.

I know you can't pick a person's friends, but you certainly don't have to be foolishly delusional about their influence over your husbands. Why wouldn't we judge them when we know for a fact their friend has been married and divorced several times, have five kids by five different women and has a different woman in his house almost on a daily basis! What does that say about him? Let me see... uhm, dirty, dingy, nasty DOG comes to mind! We judge what we see and what we see is despicable behavior. Question, do you think if your man went out with three of his friends and there are four hoochies looking for a good time that your man is not going to take up the slack? I have no doubt he will, if only to hold a certain image in front of his friends. I have heard a man say that he once only asked for a female's phone number because he was dared by his friends to do so; and what does his "married" dumb ass do? He shows no respect for his wife and goes over and asks for the number. First of all, his dumb as should not indulge in childish games and granted he could have just thrown the number away, but he used it to call this female on a regular basis. Should we women be surprised by that? Absolutely not; even though he was supposedly dared, he asked for the number; he wanted it anyway and used the "questionable" dare as an excuse to ask for it. Men don't realize that their friends hold no loyalty towards their family and could care less if they end up divorced and miserable. The children don't belong to his friends so why the hell would they be worried or have any concern for them? Stupid, silly, dumb ass rabbit, tricks are for fools! Men also don't realize that even though we don't say something about every little thing they do, we are paying attention. We can be cooking, on the phone, feeding the baby and still notice if they are doing something out of character. Women are very intuitive and CAN find that needle in a haystack if we make an attempt to do so. Something else I mentioned a bit earlier that bothers me is certain calls that a man gets on his cell phone that are somewhat suspicious. One call he'll talk in front of you laughing and joking because it's actually one of his friends and the next call he's talking like the house has been bugged by the FBI, CIA, and Russian intelligence so he goes outside to finish the conversation because, of course, it's someone he shouldn't be talking to. Ok, what "dumb" truck do they think we just fell off of? Men can't actually think we believe that would be considered an innocent phone call. My advice, follow his wagging tail right on out the door and listen up! He's going to give you this funky "what" look and you just return the gesture by giving him the "you bitch" look. The computer is another one; you're in an opposite room and he's on the computer exploring until his cold little black heart is content, but as soon as you walk in he's minimizing screens quicker than you can react to gunfire, and that's fast as hell for the average person! Of course, once again you don't say anything but you're thinking to yourself "he believes himself to be so slick, but I'm the banana peel in this marriage, I'll eventually catch him!" Going a step further, men will break your heart then walk all over it. I have not had the displeasure, thankfully, of going through this but I have people close to me that have dealt with their men making babies outside of their relationship! If that's not a relationship killer I don't know what is. The funny thing though is that some women don't just up and leave that man, they sometimes, more often than not, stick by him and give him another chance. What I don't like about that situation is that some of the women, or shall I say little girls, feel the need to hunt that other woman down and give her a piece of her mind; that anger filled outpour of rage that their spouse or boyfriend should have gotten. Trust me, I know there are some trifling, lowdown, dirty females out there but your spouse or partner has the commitment to you, not that other female. Now I can totally understand if that woman has targeted you to be the butt of her teasing, pledging to make your life miserable by harassing you and being everywhere you are and you knock her flat on her ass so she'll leave you alone is one thing, but to go and pick at that woman in my opinion is totally uncalled for because she didn't make your sorry ass man lie down with her, risk his life and yours, to create that child; it was his decision to do so. On a darker note, she also didn't force your partner to put you at risk for HIV, AIDS, or some other STD by having sex with her. Know this my ignorant little trolls for men, you can't tell someone is sick just by looking at them. What I find distasteful about some women in what some call the "baby mama drama" situation is that they will verbally berate that innocent child, saying things like "I don't care what he did, he doesn't have anything to do with the little bastard so the bitch can just stop calling telling him what the little brat needs!" Now women, you couldn't be bought any cheaper making nasty and disparaging comments about innocent children such as those. That child is innocent in the entire situation and didn't ask to be brought into this world by the mother or your man! Would I stay with my husband if this were a situation that I was confronted with? NO, NO, NO, and Hell NO, but each woman handles hurt, pain, and confrontation differently. Most men are liars by nature. Men lie about things that have no need for a lie or lie so badly that they should have saved the trip their lips and tongue just made as high as gas prices are! For instance, some cell phones make a beeping sound when the person you call are switching over to answer the second line so you ask "were you on the phone" and they flat out lie and say no. If you men lose your wives because of your infidelities, all you can do is chalk it up to a lesson learned, a lesson not to be repeated, and take care of your children but I hope like hell that you are more miserable than melancholy times ten for screwing it up! Could trust be regained after such a display of dishonesty? I think it can, but it can take several months or even years before you regain that trust. It's not going to be easy and it's also not your man's place to tell you when you should get over what he did to you or that you're being silly and holding on to the past making you feel like you're the problem. We women are entitled to take as much time as we need to get over the pain that eats away at us like a shark at bleeding flesh. Men have a tendency to do this in order to speed up the process so they can start the same cycle of lies over again. As I touched on the subject earlier, I know women who have had their men have multiple outside children on them and stay the course. My heart goes out to them because I don't believe theirs still beat the same after being hurt in such a way. The killing part is that some men will take care of their outside children and won't do anything for the children he has inside his home. Now how sick and twisted is that?! After all that, we still love our lying little dogs we call our men; it takes a lot to push us to leave them but when that time comes, there is no talking, begging, pleading or sobbing that can change our minds. Another touchy subject for me ironically is women. I, by way of nature or just by the way the wind blows do not have nor do I want a lot of female friends or acquaintances. I have three that I truly consider close friends and a few that I consider to be good people and worth some of my verbal time when I see them and the others to me are just blocking my view! Being a woman, having a daughter, mother, sisters, and nieces that I would give my life for, I can honestly say, in my opinion, women can be some of the most sneaky, spiteful, vengeful, vindictive whenches I have ever seen; and for those of you who don't know what a whench is, allow me to enlighten you: a person who exhibits massive sexual tendencies such as prostitutes, whores, etc. I know that may seem a bit harsh, especially since this book is somewhat of a venting tool to get some things off my chest, and hopefully other women's as well, about the way men treat us, but I just can't leave those happy little home wreckers out. This type of woman will strike up a conversation with you about anything or nothing in particular, try and be in more places with you to try and gain your confidence and friendship, get your number under false pretenses and end up calling you and talking to you on the phone, coming to your home and last but not least, trying to move her ass in and yours out of your home! I don't mean to sound harsh but I don't want, desire, or need the friendship, conversation, or visits to my home. I have my three close friends, seven sisters and grown nieces if I feel the need to talk to or hang out with a female. I know some of you may think these are the words of an insecure woman, but that couldn't be farther from the truth. I have learned from looking and listening, starting as a little girl, that women, some that you think are your closest friends and can tell anything, will stab you in the back, cut your throat, and do the most screaming and falling out at your funeral. Women, watch your backs and your so-called friends because some of them are like snakes, they'll slither and sneak up behind you and bite you right in the ass poisoning your system and hoping for your death; or the death of your marriage at the very least! Don't let me have to be the one to say "I told you so!" Woman's Intuition, it's a gift…use it! Now, back to those little critters we call men. I feel comfortable clumping about 70% of men into the "dog" pound because as difficult as they are to find, there really are a few good men out there and I'm not talking about the military either! That 30% that I hold out hope for are usually noted as being married, gay, in jail or dead. I don't believe that. I believe we get what we ask for and in trying to find a man that looks like Denzel Washington, Morris Chestnut, Carlos Leon or Brad Pitt, we sometimes end up with the bottom feeders that are only looking to have sex, sleep all day, not work or help pay bills, drink alcohol for breakfast, lunch and dinner and curse and shout obscenities all day long. Can I just say that I think actor Ed Harris would be worth atleast a small migraine? I'm just kidding ladies, but I do think he's very handsome and super talented; oh, did I mention he's very handsome? I'm just having a little fun! These men we choose may be gorgeous on the outside but their insides are rotten to the core with the strong stench of dead carcasses. No one, atleast I don't, wants that in a man. This is the type of man that stays in the mirror more than you do worried about that little pimple he sees coming, an ingrown hair on his chin, or his freshly cut hair not looking as straight as he thinks it should! We as women need to learn that love is more important than looks. We should want a man that shows his mother, daughter, female family members, and any woman off the street the utmost respect; this man would more than likely be a man that would shower you with love and respect. Many women confuse being loved with getting gifts and money on a regular basis. Of course you want a man that's going to treat you like a queen but that does not mean he has to spend money all the time to do that. Some have called me spoiled and lucky but I can assure you I know the difference between the two. Being treated like a true queen means being told on a daily basis that you are loved. Time is made for you regardless to what has to be done that day. This man would turn down his friend's invitations to anything without a second thought because he would rather be with you. If you have children from another relationship he treats them as if he had fathered them himself; the same way he treats his own. We should want a man that will get in the kitchen and cook for us instead of always hearing "where's my food? What am I suppose to eat?" Sometimes you just want to say "you can eat your foot if you can get it off you lazy bastard" when they act like they are unable to do things for themselves. Men also have the ordasity to think they can hang out all day or after work, if they have a job, and come home whenever they see fit, expecting a hot cooked meal. He'll get a hot meal alright; one where the pot hits his ass upside the head as you're giving it to him! Since when has that been an acceptable part of a marriage or a long term relationship? Men seem to lose all sense of morals when they get with their buddies. Why would a man in a relationship run the risk of ruining it by trying to hang out like he's still a single man? What men fail to realize is that those so called friends of theirs don't care if their marriage ends; they don't care what type of relationship they have with their children as long as they can get and keep them in the streets. Some may even want it to end because they see he has a good thing and they want it for themselves. Sometimes I wonder if men realize they are teaching their sons to treat women the same way they treat their mothers, teaching them that there is no such thing as respect for a woman, especially when that woman is their wife. They also fail to realize they are teaching their daughters that it's ok to be disrespected; that it's ok for their man to come and go as he pleases watching their mother's play the happy housewives; most of the time with you also holding an outside job. They want us to just sit there like a good little dumb wife and take it. Well we don't have to take it! We deserve all the respect, love, and trust that a marriage or committed relationship entails and to be truly happy within that marriage or relationship. What gets under my skin is when men try and use the age old reverse psychology on you to make you feel guilty for what they are doing. Men will try and make you feel like you are the bad person by wanting them to be home more often and act like a married man; to act like they remember how to be your husband. Don't get it twisted women, you deserve for him to have his sorry ass at home with you and your children whenever you want him to be there! That is exactly where he is supposed to be, and he should be happy about being there! Men are like little children; they are so easily influenced by their friends that you wonder if they really remember that they are adults and married for that matter! Men get to a point where they say things like "what's wrong with me spending a few hours doing something I like to do?" You're standing there thinking, ok there's twenty four hours in a day; you spend nine to ten hours at work leaving about fourteen. You go to the gym to work-out, or atleast that's what you tell us you're doing because we see no difference in the size of that keg you call a stomach, for three to four hours leaving around ten hours. You sleep atleast six to seven hours a night to make sure you are rested enough to work. There are three maybe four hours left in the day and they have the balls to try and make us feel guilty about them staying home for those few hours; most of the time they are pre-occupied with a ball game on TV, a video game or playing poker on the computer, or having to run to the store or to put gas in the vehicle during that three to four hour time span for it to even count! This is five sometimes six days a week and they wonder why you want them home full time, atleast on their off days. Keep in mind that some men have leisure activities that they do during the week and sometimes on their off days like tournament bowling, playing on a softball team or playing in other types of sporting tournaments. This is also time away from their families and they still complain that they never have enough time to do what they want to do. They should be happy we still want to spend time with their simple-minded asses. You even have some sorry ass men that have to leave home on a daily basis to "go to their buddy's or cousin's house" to drink every single day saying "I don't want to just sit in the house and do nothing!" Well, get your ignoble as up and do some Mr. Fix it shit around the house or sit your asinine ass on the front or back porch and you won't be just sitting in the house doing nothing! As a good woman and wife, I would pose the question "what about what your family wants you to do?" Men can't see that because their too busy trying to look for the next easy piece of diseased booty that may come their way. I have also learned that when men are called on what you know they are doing, they are ready to turn your conversation into a Tyson -vs- Holifield match! They also see three shades of fire red when someone that knows the both of you say "oh, I just saw your husband going towards wherever the hell it is they may be sneaking off to." When you ask them about it, they automatically jump on the defensive with "I wasn't doing a damn thing and I don't know why they came back and told you they saw me!" What shows their guilt is that the person that saw them was in no way saying they saw something inappropriate happening, they just mentioned that they saw them in passing and blew the horn at them to acknowledge them and speak. The problem with that is your man wasn't going to tell you he was going in that direction because he had no valid reason to be doing so, especially at that particular time so he knows he needs to figure out a good lie to cover for that time frame. The funny thing is, as soon as they make eye contact with that person they know will mention seeing them, they turn those vehicles around and try and get their monkey asses back home so fast that it's almost hilarious. They immediately, on the drive home, begin thinking of the lie that they are going to tell to cover their sorry butts. Don't let them be spotted at a time they're supposed to be at work; they want to torture and kill the person that mentioned seeing them! I, for the life of me, can't wrap my mind around why men just won't say "I want a divorce because I realize I can no longer stay faithful in this marriage and instead of cheating on you, I would rather we separate on good or atleast descent terms; I owe you atleast that much respect." I guess that's too much like right for them to act like men and fess up to their true feelings and just tell us how they feel. The thing is they know they really don't want to let go knowing some other man is going to enjoy that soft, sweet, delectable piece of chocolate or vanilla cake they called their wife! The thing is men want to have their cake and eat it too! My thinking is that there are several reasons why they would rather step out on their wife than to divorce her like, not wanting to pay child support or alimony, not having someone there to be their personal fool, and last but not least not even wanting to imagine the possibility of another man pleasing and treating their wives like a real woman. Men also have this strange idea that they can tell us how to dress. Men would have us dress like we're wearing a nun's uniform than to have us wear clothes that actually fit because they don't want the next man looking at us when all the while they are checking out the next man's woman. They want us looking like old maids, hoping no other man will pay any attention to us. This strengthens their already over rated male egos and keeps them feeling secure that we won't leave them for another man because they think no other man will have us! I say to you women, don't go out looking like a stripper or a part time street walker, but definitely put on your nice clothing that accentuates what you have and feel good when you do because when that confidence shines through men, including your own, will most certainly pick up on it. We don't do this as a way of trying to cheat, but rather as a way of feeling good about ourselves, even though our husbands don't seem to feel the same way. This may sound like a total untruth but it couldn't be closer to the truth. I witnessed, on a reality type television show, where a man was caught cheating on his wife of more than ten years and his excuse was after screwing the same thing for so many years, he wanted to screw something new!" I cleaned the language up but he didn't bite his tongue or hesitate when he said it!

He looked his wife square in the face and said it like he was saying "I Love You." He even laughed about the situation! I don't know how he walked away without her leaving his face looking like he had been in a boxing match with ten professional contenders fighting against him alone, but he did; go figure! I say these things, you should know my imagination for metaphors by now, but I don't condone violence unless it's self defense of some kind. I would not encourage any woman to become violent with her man or with the other woman that is caught with him because there is nothing more pitiful than two women fighting over a lackluster ass man that in the end is still going to do what he wants to do! Now don't mistake being non-violent with allowing your husband or his mistress to physically attack you because then it becomes a whole other situation; you are to vehemently defend yourself against any and all attacks directed towards you, but make sure that's the reason you are doing it. Don't give your husband or the other female the satisfaction of watching you make a fool of yourself in private or especially in public. You don't want to draw a crowd and have all your dirty laundry aired to the general public; telling your husband you hate him and you want him to get his few rags and get the hell out because you will never take him back, all to have the same people see you and him together a few days later like the situation never happened. While I'm not saying you should really care about what outsiders think of you for deciding to try and make your marriage work, you don't want to come off looking like a weak fool that lets her man walk all over her and treat her with as much disrespect as possible and you seem to love him more each time he does it. It's not about saving face either; it's about not being his fool. It's about being his wife, the person he's supposed to love more than anything or anyone in this world. A lot of times we women forget that. Ladies, we don't have to accept being mistreated that way. Let's stop the cycle of being abused while working to strengthen our self respect, self worth and self esteem. We women also find ourselves torn sometimes between feeling guilty and feeling like a lady. What I mean by that is when you have other men compliment you on something as small as your earrings or as big as how nice you look in the outfit you have on; you feel guilty for liking the attention; something your husband should be giving you. I wonder if a natural blonde changed her hair color to a beautiful Asian black, or vice versa if her husband would even notice; I know that's an extreme example, but men seem to look right through instead of at their wives. We feel guilty for wanting to feel wanted; we allow ourselves to feel like we are cheating because we take that compliment and smile with it the rest of the day. We tend to feel like we're leading the man on by smiling and saying "thank you" when our husbands make it a daily ritual to tell every other woman but us those very same things! Women, don't feel guilty, feel good that other men still see you as worthy of being complimented. Feel good that even though your husband has forgotten how to notice, there are still men out there that haven't. Why should we have to feel like second class citizens in our own homes because our husbands have forgotten who we are? For a lot of us women, when put in this type of situation, we allow ourselves to feel like less than a woman; like we've done something to deserve being treated this way. We need to understand that sometimes this is what men want; for us to walk with our heads hanging down and sit slouched over with poor posture like we don't care about ourselves because like I said before, this is what keeps their egos flying high. We see our men gawk at the television when they see women portrayed as symbols of sex, losing a piece of their dignity with every time they twirl their butts in front of the camera in a cheapening music video, or at a female passing by in nothing but her ten year old daughter's outfit and compare you to them, telling you that you need to be more like the them or the "video vixens" is what they like to call themselves. I just call them cheap pieces of meat that will sell their dignity for a few dollars and fifteen minutes of fame. All the while you are thinking "I would never want to do or be that; my mother and father would disown my ass!" I don't want to show my butt to anyone but you, granted you don't deserve to see it most of the time and there are many other men out there that would like to see it, but I still only want to show it to you...for now atleast! Now I don't mean things that may be sexual in nature done by a "real actress" and done tastefully and with some class. I also don't want my opinion to be mistaken for any type of envy or jealousy because my thinking is really "to each his own" because if the truth be told, any of us can get in front of a camera and shake our asses if we thought that would make us more of a woman, but it doesn't; it makes us something other than the type of respectful women we are striving to be seen as and to have men look at us in a respectful way. We should also understand that we don't "need" a man. I have found that some women seem to deteriorate if they don't have a man in their life or in their beds. These women use the excuse "I don't like being by myself;" what's the alternative, being with a man that shows you zero respect just so you'll be able to say "I have a man?" I have also found that some women make excuses for men whose attitude's reek of manure. When we find ourselves in this situation, the best thing to be is without a man. We need to use this alone time to find that "me" inside that helps us understand why we constantly repeat the cycle of failed relationship after relationship. It's like a swinging door that men constantly use to enter and tell you all the little things you think you need to hear, have their way with you, and walk out telling their friends all the things that they have no business hearing. We should not spread ourselves so thin or sell ourselves so short; we are much more than a trophy or a bed partner. Ask yourself these question ladies, "How many times have you, after sleeping with a man, felt like it has fixed whatever was broken inside of you?" Has it boosted your self esteem or made you feel even more cheap and used than before? My guess is that you probably ended up feeling worse than before. We need to take enough time, without a man, to figure out who we are and if we're the person we want to be because sleeping with a man is not going to help us women find that person; it will only cheapen you as a woman and push you further into the lonesome abyss that you are already in. Again, you don't want to be known as the free ride that expects nothing in return. That's not love, that's just sex! Remember, some men will tell us anything to try and get in our pants and then brush us off with one of the oldest lines in the book like "it's not you, it's me; this was just the wrong time for us so maybe we just need some time apart to breathe a little!" Yeah right, you were easy prey for him; he got in your panties too quick and easy and found a way to get rid of you! They also have no problem giving all the intimate details of the fling to anyone who will listen. We should have far more respect for ourselves than that.

We women sometimes make bad choices and pick the wrong guys; we often pick the guy we want to be with and not the guy that's good for us to be with. There's a saying that I think us women should always remember, "Those who do not remember the past are condemned to repeat it!" My interpretation of that statement is that some of us women jump from man to man, relationship to relationship, not giving ourselves any time in between to feel the pain of a relationship that has ended and in our vulnerable state, we feel like if we hurriedly replace the man from the failed relationship we won't have a chance to feel any pain. To me, that's like mixing alcohol and sleeping pills; it's potentially fatal. The only thing this does is destroy our self worth and self respect so that other's will see us in the same light we place ourselves in; the light that shows a very cheap and tawdry image of ourselves. I have also found that men who can't get out of their homes as much as they would like to, find companionship in their workplace with some of their female co-workers. You know the "office affair" as they call it. I think that is the most sneaky and underhanded way a man can find to cheat on his wife. Most of us watch our man leave the house thinking he's going to work to do a job and come home to us and our families; well set yourself up for that thing called "a rude awakening." Our men, in front of all their other co-workers, make sure to take their breaks at the same time as the whench they've singled out. They spend the family's money buying her lunch. They sit over in corners snickering and giggling about the things they're doing behind his wife's, and very possibly her husband's, back. For a long time, I thought it was just me; then I learned it's not because I have sisters, nieces, friends, acquaintances, and have heard of other women that feel the same way. We're the majority so I can't understand why a man would feel that it's an appropriate thing to do while trying to make sure their wives don't find out about it. There are also some men out there that don't care. They don't even attempt to hide the affair because they know their wives will either not believe it or like I mentioned earlier, be good little girls and just take it! Men don't volunteer to tell their wives about their "lunch break" partner because they know they're doing wrong! How about when they tell you they are going out of town, alone, on a business trip and you call his office all to find out "Greg and Jennifer, his assistant, has already left for the airport. Why did he lie? Maybe because he and his assistant are having an affair and will be using part of the business trip as a cozy little vacation sneak away! Some may say they don't tell because their wives are already insecure; that bullshit and they know it. I honestly feel they don't tell because of their own guilt and track record of deception. I would really like for a man to tell me, and have it make some type of sense, why they cheat. Exactly what is it? Is it long hair, short hair, light complexion, dark complexion, rail thin, curvy or healthier, what she drives or doesn't drive, where she works, who she knows, blonde hair, black hair, brown hair, red hair, where she lives or is it just the way she talks that makes them cheat? It sure as hell isn't her anatomy because she has the exact same things as your wife; maybe with a few fake enhancements, but still the same thing! Why can't you men be satisfied with who you fell in love with; the woman waiting at home for you everyday? As I mentioned earlier, men can't stand the thought of another man pleasing their woman. If we, by the way the wind blows, fall weak and find ourselves in a compromising situation that could possibly lead to us doing something like…cheat, that same man of yours that has cheated on you countless times and without any regret, will be more than outdone; he will start quoting the bible, the self righteous bastard, and asking questions such as "why are you doing this, how could you do this to me, I thought you loved me?" All of these questions before he tries to physically assault you or the man you were with. Your answer should be 'I don't know why I did it, maybe for the same reasons you did it to me!" Of course he'll say "what the fuck do you mean by that?" Leave his ass guessing. Remember that feeble mind I mentioned? It will start spinning around on him like a carousel because he would not know how to respond to that. He will more than likely stutter, curse, yell, blink uncontrollably, and probably break a couple things, but he still won't have a response for you. Men can't handle a real woman; they want a submissive woman that will play along with their silly games and not demand any kind of respect within their relationship. Men want for us to be "good little dumb girls" for them. Well, I wasn't too good at being a good little girl when I was a little girl, I had a very strong opinion about everything back then too, so chances are I'm not going to play that role all too well now! Like I said, I had an opinion about most things then and that definitely has not changed. I still question motives and intentions of people that try and get close to me and I always try and dodge the "gotcha" bullet. That's the bullet that men shoot out at you and if you're not watching carefully and it will hit you where it hurts the most; right in the heart! I'm a real woman that can't stand a dog ass man or his cheating ways! Women help me out here if you can because this is something that I never could, and still can't, understand about men. Why is it when men say they are going one place and will be there for a certain amount of time and you let that amount of time, plus some, pass and you call them on their cell phones and are like "where are you, did you decide to stay longer?" They then come back with this line, "oh, I was on my way home and passed by Tyrone's place and saw him and a couple more guys standing outside and decided to stop for a while and drink a few beers." Correct me if I'm wrong ladies, but do you agree that he could have taken that same cell phone that you just called him on to call you and let you know he had changed his plans and decided to do something else, something other than what he told you. You know, show you a little fucking respect! Why the hell is it so hard for them to squeeze just a little respect out of their sorry asses and call and say "hey babe, I'm going to stop by Tyrone's house for about an hour or so and throw back a couple beers, unless you had plans?" Truth be known, first of all he had no reason to drive by Tyrone's house to get his dumb ass home! There were three or four other directions he could have taken to get home; none of which would have taken him out of the way in the slightest! He had every intention of going that way for the sole purpose of stopping and spending more time out of the house; with Tyrone…maybe, maybe not! I know I can't be the only woman that doesn't appreciate the constant lies a man will try and feed you, after a while that bullshit is going to start coming back up. Why can't they just be straight forward about their plans and if they should change, just open their damned mouths and tell us before we have to call their ignorant asses and find out? What will he do when he gets his ass home? Play a couple games on the computer while stuffing that fat ass baby carrying belly even more and then go to straight to sleep without a conversation or word because he has to go to work and he's spent all his waking hours with everyone but you and his kids! Like I said before, what a wonderful husband and father. You can't just buy that quality of husband; probably because they would rot and spoil on the shelves because what woman in their right mind would pay for misery? Most of these character flaws men have come with the territory, but some men love to push that big red button that says "DO NOT PUSH!" They love to see just how much you can take; just how much they can get away with before you turn into the Kraken and smash their bodies to bits! Yeah, I have a big imagination but living with a man you have to be able to laugh about things because otherwise you will live in utter grief and that's an awful place to be. I was dropped in it a couple times myself but found the help to crawl out, hopefully never to return! Some men have found a way to try and justify being unfaithful to their wives. They would have us believe that it's just part of a man's social makeup for their eyes to wander and for them to cheat! Now if anyone out there truly believes that, I have a piece of land in the twilight zone I want to sell to you! We are supposed to believe men are biologically inclined to cheat; that they can't help themselves. Now that's a bunch of crap if there's ever been such a thing. We're also to believe that men and their sneaky little cronies lose all sense of control when they have a bit too much to drink and that's supposed to excuse them for the wrong that they do. I don't care how much a person has to drink; it's no excuse to cheat. If you know you can't handle or control your attitude when you drink, then your weak minded, ill-informed ass shouldn't be drinking! The bottom line is cheating is wrong and it hurts the person that you are supposed to love; it puts that person in a situation that they should never have had to be in. Men also love to use the excuse that they cheat because their wives are not as interested in sex as they are. If that's the case, one of my sisters put it best as we were joking around once and said "for all those men that feel they don't get enough sex from their wives, go in the bathroom and whack at it until you're satisfied!" You wanting to have sex six times a week and she only wants to have sex four times a week does NOT entitle you to go out and not only risk your pitiful ass life, but endanger hers as well. What the hell gives you the right to cheat and put her life at risk? Some men use the tired old line saying "I just needed a change." I say "well go right ahead and change your raggedy ass underwear and maybe you'll look better to us and we'll want to have sex more once you do!" That line is so old and tired; the people during the dinosaur age probably used it. Men will use any excuse they think might hold a ring of truth to it so that they can step out on their wives and be forgiven for doing so. I'm not oblivious to the fact that adultery has been around long before my thirty four years here and will most definitely be around for longer than my next thirty four years, but that still does not make it right. Like that song by the Jones Girls that says it better than I ever could "you're gonna make me love somebody else, if you keep on treating me the way you do." Like they say "I don't wanna do it, I don't wanna do it" but hey, if that's what you men want far be it for us to disappoint you! Any woman that is not familiar with that song hurry up and get to know it! Some of us, supposedly being church going, God fearing people will praise monogamy during church service and abolish it as soon as they step out in a club, hear one of those "drop it like it's hot" songs and see someone they think will "give it up" just because of conversation and make a race towards them! This is a nation full of heathens that claim to love God, his word, and to be devout followers and still shame him by circling the block on their wives. Some men will go so far as to say "atleast I'm not cheating with anyone she might know; my friend lives in another town!" What kind of sick logic is that? A woman doesn't have to know who her husband is cheating on her with for it to hurt her, expose her to Aids, and ruin their family. It's wrong and there is no way to make it right; no way to make it acceptable behavior. Don't get me wrong, I don't profess to be a saint; I tell people I'm a saved sinner! I have done my share of selfishly delightful things, but what sets me, and others like me, apart is that we learned from the mistakes we made. OK, this one is the most disgusting, in my opinion atleast, by far; a man uses the excuse that he's not cheating on his wife because he's only having the other woman perform oral sex on him because his wife doesn't do it! I know there are women out there that enjoy this act and then there are some that are like me; we're like 7up with caffeine, never had it, never will! I've never had, don't have now and never will have the urge to perform that act; once again, to each his own. It's just not a part of my make up. I have no vitamin deficiencies that performing that act will help to increase! I just made myself laugh with that bit of humor! Seriously though, men shouldn't try and force their wives to do things if they are not turned on by it and it disgusts them more than having to bathe in a heaping pile of liquid horse manure! Not having this included in the sexual part of your marriage is still not a reason to cheat. Nowhere does it say that this is a must in a marriage because if it were, I wouldn't be married! By the way, even if that is the only act performed between you and another woman, to which I would never believe, it is still cheating. There is no way, shape, or form it can be changed into to make it anything else. I honestly believe some men cheat because it is learned behavior. You, as a young child, are riding with your father and walk inside the home of another woman and see him kiss and fondle her has to be confusing; but as you get older you realize it was just your father being what he may refer to as "a man's man" and dishonoring his vows to your mother. You may hear your mother and father arguing about his philandering and even though they scream and yell, your mother doesn't leave. Your mother ignores it as if it's a nagging cough like it will go away but it never does. Looking up to your father, you may think "it can't be wrong if he's doing it" or "my mother didn't leave so why would my wife leave me?" That sets the stage for you as an adulterer. I have learned that most women are careful of what they do in front of their children, not speaking in terms of cheating, but just their everyday behavior. Women, more so than men, talk to their children about the rights and wrongs of life and being in a relationship; what will make it stronger and what will destroy it. We need to be able to trust in our husbands love and in the belief that they would never cheat on us and put our lives or family life in jeopardy. Men play a major roll in keeping their families together by comforting their spouses with encouragement that they are happy in the marriage, their strong belief in fidelity, and that nothing could or would ever cause them to break their marriage vows to us. This can't be just a song and dance, it has to be real and you have to be respectful of your wives. I have had men say that "they cheat because their wives don't turn them on anymore or all she does is bitch, moan, and nag." Once again, I say that is what a divorce is for. If you don't love your wife and family enough to find out why she bitches, which is most likely because of something you are doing, or to let her know what turns you on, as long as it doesn't turn her off, and give your marriage a chance you always have the option of filing for a divorce. I know what you're probably thinking "it's cheaper to keep her" but that is definitely not the case these days. That woman can take you for a ride around the monopoly board and rack up by taking the kids, her rightful share of the assets, properties, and having you go straight to jail if you don't follow the laws! That's just a metaphor of course, but women do have choices these days and those choices are backed by a court system. A lot of times you men deserve to lose more than just some of your assets, you deserve to have to give up your self-respect and your dignity for treating your wives in such a shameful manner. When you have children involved, you cause pain to not only your wife but to them as well. You have just broken the one thing in their life that they probably believed was stable and unbreakable. When they're at a certain age, you force them to choose between you and their mother as far as living arrangements. You force undo strain on an already hurt wife and even more on children that are confused and don't want to have to choose. It's a sad day and an even sorrier father that would put his family in that situation because he couldn't keep his little Vienna sausage sized penis in his pants outside of home. Don't even get me started on the men that brings outside women into the sanctity of their marital bedrooms! There are no words available to describe that kind of man. We women sometimes find ourselves so bogged down by the hurt and disappointments that life can throw at us that we become weak and sometimes even suicidal. None of us women are above feeling like we just can't take anymore and want to give up sometimes. As I stated previously, we all deal with pain differently; it's those women that you feel the most for because they have sunk their entire self into being their husband's wife. There's an old saying and throughout the years I have learned that it is so very true; "never put all your eggs in one basket!" This is not to say put some of you're your eggs in another man's basket, but rather hold on to them so that you won't be left holding an empty basket! Men are like thieves in the night. They will sneak up behind you and cut your heart out with the very knife that you cut your wedding cake with. After catching you off guard with that, they tell you "It's not anyone else, but I just don't know if I want to be with you anymore." How do you put yourself back together after being axed into pieces like that? What are you supposed to say? How are you supposed to react to that? Like I said before, men want to have their cake and eat it too; the heartless little shitheads! How can he hold a straight face and tell you he doesn't love you but he doesn't want you two to split up either? Men can be some strange spineless creatures the majority of the time and acting in such a way only proves what I have been saying all along; men can't stand the thought of another man pleasing his now or his ex while he runs around with his next! They come up with all these stupid tactics to be able to freely roam the streets telling you things like "I just need some time to think or I'm not doing anything wrong, I'm just hanging out with the fellas." What their obtuse and witless asses don't seem to realize is that being away from your family so much is wrong. Come on, do you think he's going to be that calm and nonchalant about you going out with the girls, especially if his perception of one or more of them is that they are whores? Hell no; he's going to think of every legitimate sounding excuse under the sun to keep your ass at home. His ass will be too scared you have found a friend that's packing more of a "juicy jumbo" than a Vienna sausage and he definitely won't want you humming the "I feel so very good" song around him with that smile that just won't go away! Another one of those tell-tell signs are when he always has to work overtime. That usually means he has met someone on the following shift that he's trying to give some time to or maybe not even being at work for that fact! One way to fix that like I said earlier, call his ass on the company line to make sure he has his ass there. Another way ladies is to check your man's pay stub; if there's only eighty hours on there and you know he told you he was working overtime and should have ninety hours, he damn well better have a good reason for why the hell the other ten hours of pay are not on his check! Like I've said before, men have no sense of respect for their wives. You can have fifteen different family members, your best friends, an ex, and someone who just wants to tell everything they see and hear at a gathering and yet some men are so unbelievably bold, they still try and cheat on you there knowing full well you will be told atleast ninety-five percent of what went on by someone there within an hour of seeing his stupefied ass. Besides that, how could he give your family reason to question his sincerity and commitment to you, in public? Just a low-down, backstabbing, dirty, dingy, nasty ol' mutt of a man! Men don't care that cheating hurts their wives and any children involved; they care more about how many sluts they can sex rather than how they are negatively affecting their family. The bible says "Husbands, go all out in your love for your wives, exactly as Christ did for the church." How many men do you think actually pay attention to that? How many actually know the verse for that matter. Men don't know how to pamper their wives anymore. They lose all sense of romance when they know they've captured your heart and you only have eyes for them. What about just saying "I love you" as you're walking pass your wife? Is that so hard for you brainless screw-ups to do? There are plenty things you can do to rekindle the love and spark in your relationship, starting with dumping your buddies and your very regular outings to a very, very minimum amount of time, the need to drink beer like it's water and ride the streets as though you're looking for hookers. You can also do the laundry, iron her clothes, run her a nice warm bubble bath, cook dinner, and rub her feet or any of the things that got her to love you in the first place. Another quote from the bible; men should be the head of the household; some men take that too literal and too far! You don't have to act like a big, dumb, domineering jerk that wrestles his wife into submission. Stop the argument before it starts, admit when you're wrong, give in to end the argument sometimes, even if you feel you were 100% right because what good is that going to do if you lose the woman you love to a point on a scorecard? Stop trying to push your weight around; these days we push back…hard! Some men seem to think they set the sun and hang the moon with their prideful attitudes. Marriage is sometimes like running a fifty mile marathon; you're tired, sweaty, your back is hurting, muscles are aching, feet are burning, your vision is getting blurry and just when you think you have had enough and can't take anymore, you find that extra burst of energy to keep you going. You have to be willing to fight through the bad to get to the good. Men, If you've found yourself rummaging through the bad looking for the good, put your glasses on because it's there watching you just waiting to be found. Men, don't you know if your woman sees you going all out for her, giving her gifts, something as simple as a flower or a little note, actually listening to her instead of the TV, spending time with her, doing things before she has a chance to ask you to do them or before she does them herself, don't you know she'll love that and you even more for it? Don't you want your wife to be happy? Your time is not your own, it belongs to your wife and children and you men need to realize and understand that. You are given this life, yeah, the one you are wasting, to find a soul mate and bring joy into your lives together, not misery to both of yours. What's wrong with grocery shopping together, taking a brief stroll to catch some fresh air, actually finding time to just talk about anything or nothing just to have some alone time together? I promise it won't kill you; maybe your buddies, but not you! As a man, your goal should be to make your wife feel cherished. Treat your wife as if she were the best catch in the world, because she should be to you! You are supposed to treat your wives as if they were born from the flesh of Jesus Christ himself. Some men can also take a lesson in humility. They need to be more careful and aware of what they say and how they treat their wives. Some even try and humiliate and their wives in front of their friends to try and make themselves look like a big man; well sorry fellas that doesn't make you a man, it makes you a weak little boy crying out for attention by puffing yourself up and trying to put your wife down. A marriage is a work of God and should be treated as such. There are some of us out there, not me of course, that feel like if you let your man run wild he'll get the boy out of his system and come back home a man and settle down with you, but would you actually want him after all of that? Goodness, he could have fleas and ticks after all that barking around. Like the saying goes, you lie with dogs you get up with fleas! Most of their behavior is deplorable and has no justification what-so-ever except for the fact that they are inhuman animals. Some men will go as far as to say "men cheat, it's who we are, it's in our nature to cheat, it's a part of our natural make up and therefore we can't stop." Of course I, along with the rest of you women, should find that to be so far fetched that they can't actually believe it and I can't actually believe they parted their lips wider than God parted the Red Sea to speak it! There is no genetic flaw or extra gene that makes a man a cheating liar; it's learned behavior and it's wrong. It's their insidious nature that makes them that way. Now let's flip the script for a minute, turn the tables on them for quick thought. What do you think your man would say, or do for that matter, if you went to him after he found out you had been unfaithful and said "I couldn't help myself; he makes me feel like a real woman in bed and I don't want to lose him so deal with it or leave!" It doesn't take too much stretching of the imagination to figure out during his dramatic imitation of rage that he isn't buying it and doesn't want any part of it. What I'm trying to understand is why it's ok for a man to cheat like their putting miles on a car but a woman can have one moment of weakness, because her man is never around of course, and makes what she truly feels was a mistake, but in his eyes you have just blew up the statue of liberty, made an attempt on the President's life, invited Osama Bin Laden to your home for dinner, and did a string of bank robberies blaming it all on him? What you have actually done is put a dent in his manhood and took back some of the power you gave him over you. I'm still not saying cheating either way is acceptable, but sometimes a girl's gotta do what a girl's gotta do! There's a quote by Ralph Waldo Emerson that says "Knowledge is the antidote to fear." I take this to mean, in this area of discussion, that we are sometimes afraid to find out what we already know to be true instead of embracing the truth and dealing with it head on. We know when our men are acting up; we can feel it deep down in our bones, but like I have said before we turn a blind eye and a deaf ear to the truth sometimes because it hurts too bad to face it. We need to take this knowledge and realize that this person, causing us so much pain, is just a man! He's not a God, a demigod, or any other all powerful that can take "you" from yourself! When he's gone and you've moved on, he's still going to be that same thorn that was in your side except you gathered the strength and smarts to pull him out, treat the wound and toss him in the trash where he belongs. Let that problem go and move on; let one of those other women, who also likes to play Russian roulette with their lives, have him because you know first hand that he's no catch; he's a snake ready to shed his outer layer of skin laying in wait to strike and feed! That's what men do; they feed on your insecurities, self doubt and your love for them to make sure they get their way and you stick around to be their flunky! Yeah I said it, flunky; their servant and personal fool! We are better than that ladies and as soon as we start showing them that, they'll start respecting that! Some men think because they pay the bills that this entitles them to walk all over you and some of us take it because we have been that housewife and mother for so long we don't feel like we can do anything else. We ARE the stronger of the two species and we can do anything we set our very capable minds to do. We just have to give ourselves a little credit and a little motivational pep talk sometimes to get ourselves started; the rest will just fall into place. I will admit my own husband and I have bumped heads on several occasions about his drinking buddies and the time he spends with them; it's totally disrespectful and extremely selfish for a man, especially a married one, to always think of himself and he wants first without any regard for his family's feelings! It's also disrespectful to the other wives and children that have husband's whom are out of the house regularly because one of the group buddies decides "it time to go hunting again;" and I don't mean for deer meat either! Though we love each other immensely, we'll see whether life keeps us on the same path or split us up at a fork in the road. Life is what we make of it, good or bad. The thing of it is, it's not anything hard; it's not a test, you can definitely flunk it, but it's not a test. It's just a matter of being the type of man that you would have your daughter, mother, or sister live their lives with! Kind of takes the fun out of being a dog for you men, barking and scratching at those chicken-head fleas when you include them doesn't it? I have a question for you ladies and I want you to really think about it before you answer and do so honestly. There is this guy looking and smelling so very good, driving his 2007 BMW, never having less than five thousand dollars of spending money in his pocket at a time, living in the most immaculate condo you have ever seen and he says "he wants nothing more than to be with you;" the catch is, he sells and manufactures illegal drugs for a living. On the other hand you have this ordinary guy, nice looking, but not over the top, with a heart of gold, living in a modest home that he's worked so hard to save for and start buying, driving a Toyota, and has the most genuine and sincere smile you have ever seen and he says "I have nothing to offer but blood, toil, tears and sweat", (Winston Churchill) meaning he's going to work extremely hard and do whatever it takes to 'legally" take care of you; the catch is he works five to six days a week, making ten dollars an hour slinging trash in the back of a garbage truck. Which of the two men do you find most appealing? I'm going to go out on a limb and say the majority of you would choose completely opposite from me and pick the drug dealer! Was I right? If you dance with the devil ladies you are bound to get burned. What attracts some of us to the so called "bad boy" type? I have never understood it and have never been interested in them. Some of us women are so caught up in having Prada bags, Jimmy Choo shoes, Versace outfits, personal hairstylists, and money to blow that we pass up happiness for shopping sprees. All those material things mentioned above are nice if you can afford them and they come at a much cheaper price than your self respect and dignity! I personally don't think any amount of money could take the place of being in a healthy and happy relationship where you are both content and happy just being together and wouldn't want to be anywhere or with anybody else. Some men feel if they feed a woman enough crap, she'll acquire a taste for it. There are some of us women out there that are so happy to have money to burn that we take crap in by the mouthfuls and smile the whole while it's going down. I can honestly say I have not acquired a taste for it and am quite certain I never will. If I had to choose, I would definitely dish it out instead of taking it in. One saying that I really hate is "what she doesn't know won't hurt her." That's a tired ol' line men and some skanky women love to use. Well let me make one thing perfectly clear to you testosterone driven mongrels, it DOES hurt! What you men fail to realize is that when you are having an affair, your attitude and demeanor towards your wife and family changes and it is very noticeable to the women that has to or chooses to endure it. Women can tell when you change in that way; your behavior becomes skullduggery, distant, ill-tempered, mean spirited and cold. Not only does the wife suffer this cruelty, but the children also fall victim to your deceitful ways as well. You stop spending time with them, you stop talking to them, and you become less and less interested in what they are doing and who they are becoming because your mind is so wrapped up in your buddies and the other woman. I also find it disgusting when a child has to constantly ask, "Where's daddy?" This happens to children on an almost daily basis and it makes no sense whatsoever to me that a father is gone that much from his kids that they can only ask and wonder where he is. It's also a pitiful day when one of your children catches you or finds out you're defiling your marriage and stepping out on their mother; I will say it again, some men, that will introduce their children to their mistress or don't try and hide the affair, causes considerable trouble for their family and confusion for the child. This does a lot of mental and emotional damage to your children in the long run that they, not you, will pay for. Do you even care? How can you expect that child to have the same level of love and respect for you that they had prior to finding out that you, their father, is not the man they thought he was? Again, what is so hard about saying "I want out of the marriage or just fulfilling your commitments as a good, decent, and honest husband?" Is it alimony or child support payments that keep you from leaving? If that is the case, you're even more pathetic than I could have imagined. You would rather torture your family in their everyday lives with your deceptions and break their hearts if they find out about your extramarital affair(s) just to keep a few dollars in your pocket. Can you become any less of a man? You men need to straighten up and fly right! You want and expect so much from your marriage but are putting nothing into it. That's not fair to your wife or your children. A marriage is about two people not just one! The affair you are having seems so good right now; it's exciting, different, passionate, and it's wrong! The affair is starting out just as your relationship and eventual marriage did; everything was so perfect and easy going in the beginning. Well I'm sorry to burst your bubble men, but things change! They don't necessarily change for the worse but they do change with time. You have no real ties to your mistress so cheating seems almost better than winning the lottery! What about your wife? She is the one that gave you your children, cleans your house, cooks your meals, washes your clothes, makes your appointments, takes care of your kids, helps them with their homework, takes them to their appointments, meets with their teachers, make sure they're taken care of when they are sick, and is an all around parent, a "real" woman! How can your outside tramp compare to that? You sorry, pitiful and pathetic canines, who do you think would clean up your vomit if you're sick, wash and wipe your ass if you couldn't, would bend over backwards to get you to the hospital or to an appointment if needed? Who do you think would do all this, take care of your kids, and not complain about one single bit of it? That crown, my pissant men, belongs on the head of your wives! You men also have the ordasity to look down on your wives because they don't pile on a face full of make-up everyday, pull their hair back in a ponytail, don't get all dressed up in heels, and her nails just happen to not be done does not make her any less of a woman. This is because your wife has your children to take care of; she has your home to take care of. When your wife does find the time to do all these things, looking far better than your cheap replica of her ever could, you don't even as much as acknowledge that she has done these things for you! Some of you men have the smallest, blackest, and coldest pieces of coal you call hearts I have ever seen. It's amazing that we even put up with ANY of the crap you put in front of us. Why do we do it? We do it because when we love, we really love; we give our heart and soul to you and the marriage and will go through hell, molten lava, high waters, up a mountain and back before we give up on you! Too bad we can't expect the same from you as our husband, our friend, our partner, and our rock. You obviously have no respect for your wives or yourselves because you spit on the promises and covenants you made to her, in front of God and both your families on that special day. You shun the knowledge that you have of right and wrong so you can do your dirty work without feeling guilty and somehow make what you are doing right in your own sick and twisted minds. One of my least favorite things a man, especially a married man, can do is to ask you why you are questioning him. What a funky, nasty, flea bitten, mangy mutt. Men feel they have the right to be able to do whatever they want and you not ask them one single question about it. Who the hell do they think they are? Men you are married; if your wife wants to play twenty questions, put your damn thinking caps on and hope like hell you get all the answers correct! The bottom line is, if you weren't doing something you had no business, in a place you had no business, or talking to someone you had no business we wouldn't have any questions to ask your devious asses about you or your fidelity! You men are not entitled to get mad and defensive because questions are asked of you about a situation "you" created and now don't know how to handle so you try and ignore it. Well chew this good enough to get it down as smoothly as possible; we are not going to just ignore it and let it go; you wouldn't extend that courtesy to us and we definitely are not going to extend it to you! Regardless of whether or not you think you owe your wife an explanation about something you did, something she heard, or something she saw, you should willingly give it to her anyway! Give it willingly without attitude, raising your voice, cursing, slamming doors, throwing things, rolling your eyes, gritting you teeth or even frowning. That comes with loving and respecting your wife and your marriage. I wish men could, for once, act like men and let their wives know what is going on in their big but surprisingly empty heads. This way there will be no need to look for solace outside of your marriage and will leave no doors open for you to let another woman traipse her frowzy ass in. Open your mouths and say what you are feeling whether its your butt is getting too big, your losing too much weight and your chest and butt is getting too flat, I don't like the perfume you wear, I like you to kiss my neck when we're together, or whatever the issue may be; it can't be fixed if you don't tell us it's broken! That's if there is anything that's actually broken; which I believe nine and a half times out of ten there isn't. This is also a two-way street men, so remember that! That same sister of mine that gives men the option to "whack at it" likes to say "men need to take "dog" obedience classes because they just can't act right; they're too wild and need to be tamed!" The majority of them act like natural born fuck ups! Sadly, the fact is that most men won't do right, just flat out refusing to; it's not that they can't, they just choose not to. Men must be willing to sacrifice some of their own wants and some of their supposed ambitions to make their marriage work. True love and respect for your wife, children and marriage involves selfless giving. Men believe they can be controlling and demanding with their wives and expect us to automatically give into their demands. That cup is not big enough to hold love along with the rest of that garbage in it. Men should not look at us as objects or possessions, but as their equals. Men should also not try and manipulate their wives into getting what they want by threatening to harm her, take the kids, or leave the marriage. That is a ruthless, selfish, cowardly and underhanded way to try and get your wife to give up her pride and dignity for the sake of the marriage. Women already take enough bullshit from men; we feel like "if he sees how much I love him, he'll stop his destructive living and become an honest family man." I would strongly advise against holding your breath for that to happen anytime soon ladies because as I've said before, men feel like if they're not having sex with more than one woman that makes them less of a man. What they don't understand is that this type of behavior cheapens them and the marriage vows they took; it undermines everything that was sacred about the marriage and the love that is supposed to be solid as a rock, but was damaged, weakened, and about to crumble because of his infidelity. It will also take time to rebuild that foundation of trust and re-strengthen the bond that brought you together initially should you both choose to try and make your marriage work. Men have a serious weakness that makes my inner bitch step forward; it's when they make and finalize plans with those raggedy, drunkard ass buddies of theirs without first discussing them with us! You see him grooming himself, taking a shower, and turning the bathroom and himself into a damn chemistry lab with all that loud ass damn cologne on; so loud it's literally screaming out to you. Of course he says nothing the entire time he's getting ready to rendezvous with his buddies, and maybe a few whores, and when you ask him where he's going he just say's "Oh, I'm going over by Pierre's house;" like his ass just forgot to mention it to you earlier. Also, I would be wiling to bet that nine times out of ten it's someone you've never even heard of so you know his tainted ass is lying! The closest his ass is to knowing a Pierre is knowing a guy named Patrick he went to school with! I come back to this again because this is, in my opinion, a major problem in a lot of marriages. Men can't grasp the fact that discussing plans with their wives doesn't make them weak, and their friends telling them they're whipped doesn't make it any better; all it does is makes the marriage shaky and vulnerable. I just don't understand their ways of thinking. I can understand if you have a mandatory meeting at work or you have to actually work overtime because someone called out. Respect for your wife and marriage means saying to your buddies "that sounds good but let me just talk it over with my wife and I'll get back to you." Men, I can't say it enough times to your dumb asses, that don't make you weak, it makes you a good and respectful husband. It says to your wife "I care more about your feelings and what you think more than anybody else." I can say this until the cows come home and it can not be stressed enough that men should not let another man, or woman, come into their marriage and help tear it apart all the while telling them what they believe should be happening within their marriage. Men have to be strong enough to say "hey, I can understand where you're coming from, but I love my wife and kids and I will not do anything to jeopardize my family's foundation." Your so called buddies are only there until the beer money runs out and your wife has left you; you are no longer fun to them because they don't want to be looking into your sad ass puppy dog eyes while you're thinking about what you lost because of them. Men are too busy worried their friends will tease them about being whipped, weak, or punked by their wives. Like I said before, men's minds are so small and feeble that they don't realize someone that really cared about them or their happiness as a friend would never ask them to do or even be involved in anything that would put his family at risk! Men know how to get another man to break because they know what would break them as a man; they know just the right buttons to push to get your man to take his marriage, kids, and years together with you and toss it up in the air and hope he catches you! Let me give you men something to think about; while you're trying to play mind games with your wife, there's always another man out there that is willing to toss the games aside and help us settle into a very loving, trusting, and honest reality! Don't be too cocky about your marriage and the feelings your wife has for you because just as you are able to step out on your marriage, she can easily find happiness elsewhere and slam the door behind you for good! Women have no problems submitting to her husband, as long as he respectfully submits to her as well. It's not about being weak because it takes a really strong person to give in when they really don't want to, but that's what it takes to help keep a marriage strong and intact. I'd like to make one thing clear; when I say "women" I don't mean those low-class sluts that jump at anything with a penis and has no problem crawling into bed with a married man. Those are not women to me; they are casualties of life; bad sluttish pieces of trash that are put here to give and keep us with a damn headache! As good as we are to our men, they have no problem taking us for granted; thinking that we will always be there for and with them no matter what happens. True as that may be sometimes, we are tired of being the low ones on the totem pole. Everybody wants a piece of your time, but you have no problem with your wife and kids always ending up at the back of that line! What kind of man does that make you? It makes you denude of any common sense whatsoever! You know you have a good woman and yet you will thrust her into the arms of another man to satisfy her because you're never there. If that should happen, and again I am not advising women to cheat on their husbands, the husband should take the bulk of the guilt for treating his wife like a worthless, unlovable servant. You either love your wife or you don't; it's that simple. If you don't love her, then let her go. Don't torture her, leading her to believe you two have a future together. Allow her to leave the relationship with some dignity. Don't wait until you have beat her down so far emotionally that she is no good for anyone, including herself and your children. If you do love her, show it; respect her as your equal and leave the cheating for the little boys because a "real man" would never do anything that could come back and cause the woman he loves any type of grief or pain. You are supposed to be her shoulder, her backbone, her rock! If you show respect to no one else, she is supposed to be given the utmost respect in every aspect of your relationship. You should want nothing more than to make her completely happy and hold her and your children so close to you that not even wind could pass through! You can't confuse having your own identity with being able to come and go as you please; you're a married man for goodness sake! You see your "homeboys" leave the house in the early morning hours and return home late at night into the early morning hours of the next day and their wives say nothing. You're on the outside looking in and it looks like they have it all, a submissive wife, children that are ok with seeing daddy for twenty to thirty minutes a day and still have home to go to when they please. If that's your idea of an ideal marriage then I feel sorry for you and the family that you are eventually going to lose. Trust me when I say everyone involved in that situation is miserable, including the man! He may seem like he's completely happy but he's not because even though he doesn't show it, he knows what he's doing to his wife and family and the more he thinks about it the more he needs to be away from them. Believe it or not, men actually do have a conscious, albeit a small one and they fight like hell to keep it at bay! They want no part of it because it makes them feel that emotion called "guilt" that gives them acid reflux, heartburn, diarrhea and all other sorts of gut wrenching illnesses that cause them pain. They can't stand that feeling! Men lie because they are void of a backbone; they want to make sure you continue to think they're being good little boys to make sure your mind never wonders to the position of cheating on them. They are cowards and want to keep living the double life that they have been living. Men tend to think they are smarter than their wives, but truth be known, they're only as smart as we allow them to be! Take this situation for instance. The husband in this couple I know had a dentist appointment to get his teeth cleaned. There are two hygienists there, one very professional and the other, who had a crush on the husband years ago and probably still do, very unprofessional. The receptionist left a very professional and straightforward reminder of his appointment but the hygienist, who shouldn't be calling in the first place, left a very unprofessional and flirtatious reminder of the husband's appointment for him. Well the wife and the husband had a small discussion about it and the wife expressed her dislike of the message and of course, the husband immediately jumped on the defensive saying "well maybe the message was not professional, but what does that have to do with me?" Maybe he needs to eat more fish, beans, whole grains; you know brain food because he was acting really damn dumb then. Well the wife, not wanting to claw his eyes out, cancelled his appointment with the flirt and rescheduled it with the professional hygienist that comes to work to do a job and not look for her next screw, all this without consulting him of course, and he was livid when he found out! I asked her what the hell does it matter that the unprofessional flirt is not cleaning your husband's teeth as long as he gets the motherfuckers cleaned? He told his wife that it was just the principal of it but she knew that was horse, cow, and bullshit! Now had the tables been turned, the husband would have asked a million questions, wanted to know who the hygienist was, and would have went to her appointment with her! So damn the fact that he didn't like his appointment changed; he's lucky she didn't change the damn doctor all together! Men have a serious problem with double standards; they think what goes for you does not go for them. They believe they have more rights that you do in the marriage. My sisters, black, white, Asian, Hispanic, Indian, Gypsy or any other ethnicity, if you've fallen asleep on that nonsense you need to wake your ass up quick, fast, and in a hurry! Don't let him make you feel like you're imagining things because you're not. His wife was right on point in believing that hygienist wants to do more than to just "clean his teeth." Let me briefly touch on another class of men; the non-working class. Ladies, what's really going on? These men sit around the house all day, refuse to baby-sit their own children while you work, and take your paycheck when you get it! Am I missing something or do you need the hell shaken out of you so you will learn some sense? Why would you want a deadbeat as a companion? Why are you paying a babysitter when the child or children's father has his unemployed ass right there? You pay the bills, buy the groceries, take care of the children's needs, and he takes the rest for himself. I don't know what planet you're from, but here on Earth it just doesn't happen that way! You don't allow yourself to be used in such a way. Like the saying goes, "I can do bad by myself." This man is not your only chance at happiness, you do have other options! The man wants to be the head of the household, let him take care of his household like a real man would. You're always lachrymose and feeling regretful because you're knowingly allowing this man to take advantage of you. You're allowing him to blame everything wrong on you and free himself of any guilt; guilt that he should rightfully be feeling for not taking care of his family as he should. Something else that bothers me is when women take on a spouse or a partner that has serious alcohol and drug addictions. Where do you think that relationship will end up? What are you trying to accomplish by cheating yourself from the beginning? I sincerely hope you're not thinking you and your love for him will change him. Well let me tell you something that you have probably already figured out; you can't change someone that doesn't want to be changed. No matter how much you love them they have to love you and themselves enough to want to change, otherwise that change will never come to pass. You constantly run into situations where he has drained the bank account, bought drugs, or gambled with his entire paycheck before making it home and now you have no money for food, bills, the children or anything else. This has happened so many times that you expect it to happen. Why would you put and keep your children in that situation? Sometimes we have to give up the things we want for the greater good and that most definitely includes giving up that problem for the sake of our children. The same thing goes for alcoholics; you're children do not need to be exposed to this type of behavior. Like I've said before, children live what they learn. I have long said that children, for the most part, are in danger of growing up living the way they were raised. If your children see you are tolerant of drugs and alcohol, they really have no reason to believe that behavior is wrong; if dad does it and mom puts up with it, or vice versa, then it must be OK or not as bad as people make it out to be. Men also know when they've pissed you off. They will walk past you a couple of times to see if you're going to say anything to them and if you don't, they come back with "what's supposed to be wrong with you this time?" As soon as you take a breath and speak your first few words he yells "I don't want to hear that shit and walks off!" I tell you what ladies, walk behind his ass screaming until you have said everything you want to say; everything that is on your mind and bothering you. You deserve to be heard and to have your concerns addressed by your husband. They will make light of your problems saying "you are overreacting" but that couldn't be farther from the truth. Men hate to be put on the spot. They hate to have to answer a question immediately that requires time for them to think up a lie; that's why they cut you off mid sentence and start yelling while walking away. Make no mistake that his brain is working overtime, probably causing him to sweat profusely and become quite dizzy, but he will have a comeback for you within a couple of minutes or so. Now we move on to what I call the mama's boy. It's a precious gift to have a loving relationship with your mothers but some men take it too far. Some men act like they can't make a decision without her input. This definitely puts you out with him. He calls her for every little thing, including discussing your sex life! This is new to you so you're thinking "what the hell is going on?" You ask him about it and he says "I have always had an open relationship with my mom and we can talk about anything." You are confused, livid, but confused and try to explain to him that that part of your relationship is off limits to his mother's or anybody else's ears. He tries to rationalize his behavior but you're not trying to hear his weird explanations. Besides the fact that his mother thinks he's royalty and she doesn't really care for or think you're good enough for him anyway, he insists on confiding the intimate details of your relationship to her and asking her opinion about every disagreement the two of you have. This woman comes into your home and rearranges things as she feels they should be and then tells you what other areas she thinks you need to improve upon. Of course by now you are about to explode but keep the peace until you are alone with your husband. As soon as you try to explain to him that you neither need nor want her coming into your home and trying to turn it into her own he just says, "she's only trying to be helpful." I'm going to leave it up to the reader's imagination what happened with her, the cast iron skillet, and his head. Its turtle charged, but the realization that the two of you don't belong together is finally settling in. Your day to breakaway is fast approaching. I have two sons so I feel like I'm entitled to speak on this subject; I just pray I don't turn out to be one of those meddling old knitters that never look up as she talks to you while rocking in her chair. And once again, drum roll please…the cell phone. I don't care how it's marinated, sliced, or chewed; that cell phone of his is your "worst" enemy! It has been the center of countless arguments and rightly so. Men believe themselves to be sneakier than snakes but we women are a modern day female version of Sam Spade, Sherlock Holmes, and Columbo all rolled up into one. We have a way of finding things out. Don't let us start networking our brains; we can tell you what color underwear the President had on during his inauguration! We have a sixth sense when men are doing wrong and we will scroll through that phone or palm pilot like we're flipping through the pages of a fashion magazine; we can see everything without slowing down! We women sometimes tend to feel a little guilty if our intuition or gut feeling is telling us something is wrong because we want to believe in our cheating little pot belly trolls, but follow your first mind. Don't let your sense of 'trust" get in the way of your common sense. Calling some of those numbers from a payphone or using *67 on some of them will tell you a lot about what that old schnauzer of yours has been up to. Men can be so sneaky in a lot of the things they do. You're innocently looking through his numbers, that's right I said innocently, and you come across names of friends like Glenn, Ron, Steve, and so on that you've never met or even heard of. Let me tell you why; because those numbers belong to Glenda, Rhonda, and Stephanie; all he did was list them under men's names close enough to their names so as not to forget them. I say you don't have any friends named Glenn, Ron, and Steve until I verify it from a payphone, a visit to our home, or through *67! Don't be fooled ladies, check his ass out. This is a list of other things that you should be weary of when it comes to your man's cell phone. If he always keeps the phone off or on vibrate when you two are together, when he walks away from you while talking on the phone, when he gives vague answers to the person on the other end of the phone like yeah, uh-huh, right, I don't know, or let me call you back later, when he keeps the phone glued to his hip after he's made it home even sleeping with it on, or when he refuses to answer the phone after one or two back to back calls his butt is got something happening that shouldn't be going on. Also if he turns into the Hulk if you answer his phone, you politely play the character roll of Medusa with her bow and arrows, beaming red eyes mind you, that turn him to stone; don't let him bully you. If he has nothing to hide, there won't be an issue of who answers his phone. Women, another sign something is wrong is when your man wants you to stop driving his vehicle, when he leaves his wallet and cell phone locked up in his vehicle, and when he tries to avoid the two of you being seen together so frequently, check him out; find out what's going on and why. Something else I hate is when you call his ass on that cell phone ten to twenty times and he says, thirty minutes later, "I must have been in a bad area because I just got the page." Women, please, please, please don't believe that shit! It took him that long because he had to get out of that other woman's bed, get dressed, and get the hell out of there. I am also not opposed to the idea of you having his ass followed. They like to call it entrapment if you set bait out for them and they bite forcefully at it, but I just call it catching his ass and getting to the bottom of the situation. Trust me, he would have done it without your assistance; he just got caught with a little help from you. Men can say what they want; it doesn't matter if, in their eyes which sometimes seem to be a bit cocked with their version of "good looking", one of the most gorgeous women wearing all but nothing approaches them and starts an inappropriate conversation for a married man, they are supposed to let her know they are married and immediately turn away. Because we are so maternal or because we have gained a little weight we stop going places and doing things. Forget it, get up and get out of the house. Call up your friends, put on some nice clothes and makeup, and get out of the house. When he decides to go somewhere, besides fishing, if that's what he's really doing, volunteer your companionship and don't take no for an answer if you really want to go. Change things up to throw his ass off. Get out of that rut you're in and that he's become accustomed to and do something different. Women, make yourselves known as his wife and better half; there is no other half unless you are referring to him. Force him to acknowledge you. Some women might say "if he doesn't want me around then I'm not going to force myself on him." I say that's the inebriated version of real logic. If you feel that way, you may as well leave the relationship now; otherwise, stop being his always transparent and never seen wife. Get out and mingle with his friends even if you don't like them; I myself had to learn that lesson. A lot of us women feel the need to get even instead of getting mad; a couple of years ago I would have egged you on in cheating on his ass to get even, but now I know better. From the day you enter a relationship, you should already have in mind what you will and won't tolerate within that relationship. You should already know what will sweeten it and what will cause it to rot. Being in a relationship is the easy part; the hard part is building and maintaining it. To build a strong foundation takes love, trust, and mutual respect for each other. A relationship will not survive if only one person is breathing life into it. It takes the pain and struggles from both to make the relationship work. Whatever you may be going through in your relationship, it's never bad enough that you can't get out! Women should also be careful not to become a pro at the rebound game. We need to give ourselves some time to readjust to being single, especially if there are kids involved. We don't need to split from our husbands and within six months have already had six or seven sexual flings! I'm not sorry to say that makes you a whore, not a woman! Close your legs and open your mind and eyes to all the positives in your life so that the negatives will not over shadow them and you end up falling victim to fast talk and no substance again. The six month mark is when, in my opinion, you should just be ready to start dating again; dating that does not include sex! We sell ourselves too short sometimes and cheapen our worth by allowing ourselves to be used by men that know when we're still hurting and still searching for the person that you lost with our ex. Men have a good nose for sniffing out a troubled heart and know just what to say to get you to let your guard and panties down and let them in to tangle your thoughts up worse that they already are. Women, we don't need a man to make us. We don't need a man to feel like a woman. We definitely don't need them to sex us up and toss us aside while we're still trying to mend a broken heart and a troubled mind after separating from someone we've spent time and had children with. This will only further discourage you and make you even more of a train wreck than you already are. We spend too much time fighting to get out of the worse to even have a chance at the better sometimes. Before rushing to the alter and jumping the broom, we need to be sure that we want to be married, that we're ready to be married, and that we want to be married to this particular person. We have to be ready to give up the partying, club hopping single life that we once loved so much. That also applies if you have children. It's alright to go out maybe once or twice a month for a few hours because once you have kids you are then a mother and not a hooker for hire. If you find yourself married and you're the only one that remembers you're married, don't allow yourself to be mistreated and run over! Have the courage to tell your husband "this behavior is not acceptable; if you want to be married then act like it but if you don't, you know your way out the door! Stand up for yourself and don't bend from your demands because if you do, you have just lost the battle and are weakening in the war. He now knows what to do or say to get you to change your mind. In the end, cheating is no joking matter. If you are cheating on your girlfriend or wife, think about what you are doing to your relationship, your kids and the person you profess to love. Look at the big picture and see that your unfaithfulness only causes heartache and pain. Cheating feels good right now so your marriage is of little concern to you, but it's only for a short while; you eventually reap what you sow! Like the old saying goes "everything that looks good to you is not good for you!" I know I have only touched on a few of the many problems that can shake the foundation of a relationship and cause it to crumble, but I hope that if any women are in any one of the above situations, they will have the strength to let go and move on. Get out of that glass house that has zero stability and can shatter and severely injure you at any time. Get out of that place that opens your life up for public scrutiny by the whole world. Be that third and smart little pig, so to speak, that built his house with a firm structure and foundation. Straw, sticks, glass, it's all the same. It has no support or safety net for you to fall back on. It can easily be destroyed and therefore should not be chosen as your place of security and comfort. Don't keep allowing yourselves to be their doormats and continue walking all over you. Open your eyes and see that if you're not being appreciated as his equal in the relationship, then you should be closing the door behind you on the way out of that relationship because no good will come of it; atleast not for you and your kids if you have been blessed with any. Before your feelings, wants, and needs should be those of your children and no child deserves to be in a loveless home with a father that has to schedule them into his calendar in order to spend time a few minutes of time with them, if he spends any at all. That shows no love for the child and little respect for the family. Men, you WILL miss your water once your well runs dry. That woman you hold so little respect for is your tall cold glass of water in the desert heat; she is the quench to your thirst, and your constant flow in the cleansing of yourself in times of need. Wake up ladies;

it's a new day if you allow it. I would also like to say to my sister's…don't allow yourselves to be some man's dumping ground. What I mean by that is don't allow some man, however crazy about him you may be, to make you nothing more than his sneak; his little freak in the night! In the eyes of God, he belongs to another woman and no good will come to either of you. I know we've all done things that we wish we could change or take back, small and large, but can't. This is, however, one of the worst ways we can cheapen our worth. You are not this man's wife or significant other; you're just his call over for sex. I can't stress to you the importance of telling him NO! When he calls you, ask him if he's calling to take you out to a nice restaurant for dinner, afterwards stopping to catch a show or a movie, and then take you home with only a "I had a nice time" and enough light to see his way back to his car; this is only if he is not committed to someone else! I know how fun it is to be young and have someone pay so much attention to you, but it's the wrong kind of attention. Force these men to respect you. If he has a woman what does he need with you? To put it plainly, besides a free sex ride and being his full time fool, NOTHING! Men show little respect to women because there's always the skank for him to fall back on. That woman who does not know how to spell, know the meaning of, and has never heard the word RESPECT! And for you filthy little skanks that like to play "chase the husband", I hope he has a wife that likes to play "smack the whore!" I believe the latter would be a really fun game to play and will also be a good eye opener, or closer, for the vile sluts in attendance! Ladies, lets take back the power we have given the men in our lives and if they refuse to straighten up and fly right, lets bid their asses a forever goodnight. Don't be his victim anymore. Women, we have become so jaded by these men, their ill intentions and contemptible lies that we seem to just accept things as they are in our relationships rather than demand that they change or we leave the idiotic dunces standing out in the cold; even though it probably wouldn't bother them because of the temperature of their ice-cube hearts. We, however, hold all the power necessary to make these men become and live as real and respectful men so let's get our act together for our own sake and well being. If that's too hard for them then send their pompous, egotistical asses packing! You don't need a sorry ass man to make you a woman. You don't need a man to determine who you are or what you are capable of. What determines who you are is the respect you hold for yourself and others; a man can't earn that respect for you because he himself barely knows the meaning of the word respect. His only role should be whether or not he's going to be a positive or a negative influence in your and your children's lives; and if he's not a positive then what the hell do you need or want with him? We real and respectable women will always come out on top; believe that! It may not always seem that way at first, but your time will come. The truth, my brothers, really does hurt doesn't it? Now, I will end on a much softer and demure note. I want to give you so-called men with a scripture from the bible to remember that should tame you and your harsh ways towards your wives. James 3:5-8 says this: "Likewise the tongue is a small part of the body, but it makes great boasts. Consider what a great forest is set on fire by a small spark. The tongue also is a fire, a world of evil among the parts of the body. It corrupts the whole person, sets the whole course of his life on fire, and is itself set on fire by hell. Consider carefully what you say to your wives before you say it; it can make a world of difference in your marriages. Allow yourselves, as hard as it may be, to become good, honest, and faithful husbands. Don't allow another man, or men, to coax you into spending your family's time outside the home; you "will" live to regret it if you do. I know a lot of you are simple-minded, but even the ones of you that are know the difference between right and wrong. It'll be a sad day, for you, when you finally realize how special your wife is and another man will be reaping the rewards of your loss. Also, your "road dogs" know how far to go in their marriage to keep it together, but make no mistake in thinking that they give anything close to a damn about yours; you may not have as much room to stretch as they do and forever fall out of your wife's reach. Again, the bible says "Thou shalt <u>love</u> thy wife with all thy heart, and shalt <u>cleave</u> unto her and none else." Remember that men; this includes your buddies as well as other females. It will save you the pain of loss, loneliness, and respect in the end. You men that turn your noses up at your wives spitefully will definitely be brought back down to reality forcefully and stagnantly watch as she leaves out the door and your life for good. While I can be a forgiving person, and Lord knows I have been over the years, I feel no sympathy for a man that puts anything or anyone before his wife and children. He's worth nothing more to me than the crap you scrape off the bottom of your shoes. I leave you with some words of wisdom compiled together as poems written by me, and some by great men, that are meant to be taken with more than just a grain of salt; more like the whole box!

**James Oppenheim:**
The foolish man seeks happiness in the distance; the wise grows it under his feet.

**Epictetus:**
It is the nature of the wise to resist pleasures, but the foolish to be a slave to them.

**Balthasar Gracian:**
A wise man gets more use from his enemies than a fool from his friends.

**H. G. Bohn:**
Wise men learn by other men's mistakes, fools by their own.

**Winston Churchill:**
Men occasionally stumble over the truth, but most of them pick themselves up and hurry off as if nothing had happened.

**Epicurus:**
Do not spoil what you have by desiring what you have not; but remember that what you now have was once among the things you only hoped for.

**Evan Esar:**
The girl with a future avoids a man with a past.

**Euripides:**
Man's best possession is a sympathetic wife.


*These quotes were written before my time and yet they still carry the sound ring of truth to them when it comes to men.

# A PRAYER FROM GOD TO MY SISTERS WHO BELIEVE:

I hear your cries
I feel your pain
But today my child
You come in from the rain
Give your hurt and sorrows to me
And with my love I will set you free
From the pain that has taken over your heart
Giving you a chance at a brand new start
While punishing the one that has done you wrong
Placing your heart back where it belongs
Next to me as I sit at my throne
And denying him entrance
To paradise in the afterlife called "home!"

# D U P L I C I T Y

I sit here contemplating why
My husband feels the need to lie
To sneak and do things behind my back
Is it because respect for me he lacks
What turned him from the man he was
That showed me overwhelming love
To this person that does oh so much wrong
And justifies it with the weight of a thong
Why does he feel the need to cheat?
And beat me down until defeat
Leaving work early to meet with her
Turning our love into a blur
Does he really believe that I'm a fool?
To take at face value his utter untruths
But as the saying goes you reap what you sow
And the punishment...well only God knows

We don't want them dead or hurt, well not too bad, but we
do want their asses to suffer for their trifling behavior!

*Kathleen Taylor-Bennett*

# S P I T T

Disgusted with your lies
Strong contempt for you
Half the man I expected
Your dishonest heart knows no truth
Nauseous with your family
Big appetite for the streets
Your envy for adulterers
Why did life let us meet?
Your flirtations with other women
And pleasures in what you do
Will make sure that what you throw out
Will come back to haunt you

When men start to howl and sniff around like the dogs they are, this is exactly what I think of them.

# P E R S O N A L   F O O L

Can I wash your clothes and cook your food
Clean your house and adjust to your moods
I'll take out the trash and cut the grass
Wash the cars and even kiss your ass
I'll work two jobs and pay the bills
Run all your errands with time to kill
I'll never get angry or lose my cool
I'm here for you...I'm your personal fool


Even though this is what they expect of us, let them
know in no uncertain terms that we will not be their
pushovers.

# B O T T L E D   U P

You're a filthy, lying piece of snake in the grass trash
I hope the slut gives you a nasty rash
I hope she takes you for every dime you have
And leave you with not even enough for a cab
Then you can choke on all the lies you told
And burn in hell with your wretched soul


Well... atleast I am honest about my feelings! ☺

# *L U C K Y*

To my brothers of oh so many races and faces, count your blessings if your marriage is without spaces. List the positives in your relationship from one to ten; I'm sure there's more, so scratch that list and do it again. Think of all the happy times, you know, the ones that seem to never be on your mind. Reach out and touch your wife's hand, and be thankful the other is not linked to another man. Give my sisters the respect they are due, and be grateful you're one of one man and not two!

# *THINK BEFORE YOU LEAP*

To my sisters whose preference is someone else's man, you need to get your shit together before you crawl out of your garbage can; because for every sister that will look the other way, there's another, like me, that will beat you blue and gray. Not because with you he creeps, but because you approached and disrespected me. Back out of the circle that you've jumped your ass in and think long and hard before you decide to do it again. To you this may be fun and games, but cross the wrong path and you'll dance a well deserved shame. Pick up your respect where you dropped it off and learn to use what little you were taught. See, chickens like you are no real threat because at the end of the day you still lack his respect!

## TEN THINGS MEN SHOULD BE GRATEFUL FOR:

1) A woman at home that loves him in spite of...

2) A woman forgiving of his past and his present

3) A woman that is his audience during laughter and his rock during pain

4) A woman that has his back in times of need

5) A woman that encourages him to succeed

6) A woman willing to stick it out instead of walking out

7) A woman willing to put her dreams on hold to help him accomplish his

8) A woman willing to pull him back up after being knocked down

9) A woman willing to sacrifice her needs for his wants

10) A woman willing to share her life with him, shortcomings and all, and take on the role of his "wife"

# *E N D    N O T E*

Some may find my honesty a bit blunt or even a little brutal within the pages of this book, but I refuse fake who I am or what I feel. I'm a heart that keeps it real. My intention is only to enlighten and enliven my sisters; not that I'm an expert on relationships because I'm not. I speak from experiences, mine and others. Some points in this book are touched on a bit more than others because I feel like those are the areas where we women seem to be at our weakest when it comes to men. I hope the words within the pages of this book open the eyes and minds of women and strengthen them enough to say, "I'm no longer going to accept being treated like anything less than a real lady." If you learn to accept this and put it into practice, men and not boys will come into your lives bringing joy, stability, and attempting nothing that will cheapen your worth as a wife, woman, or mother.

I "AM" my father's daughter!

Kathleen